HOW TO TALK EFFECTIVELY

CALM YOUR MIND SPEAK TO ANYONE
ANYWHERE AVOID AWKWARD
CONVERSATIONS & MASTER SMALL TALK
COMMUNICATION HAVE BETTER
CONVERSATIONS TO PUBLIC SPEAKING LEVEL
BY TALKING EFFECTIVELY

LEON LYONS

ABOUT THE AUTHOR

Leon Lyons is a British-born, Amazon best-selling author, a Psychological expert, and a Senior Life Coach at Mindset Mastership based in London, England.

Leo as he's known to friends used to consult global brands headquartered in central London. Although now he would say he found a more fulfilling role in life: coaching clients from around the world, changing lives for the better, and when he's not traveling or surviving global pandemics, he also writes about how success can happen.

We're in the changing lives business.

SCAN ME FOR A BONUS

https://bonus.mindsetmastership.com/talk-effectively

DON'T MISS THIS! YOUR GUIDE TO INCREASING SELF-CONFIDENCE

Introducing *Increase Self-Confidence*.

This short but powerful eBook covers a wide range of topics to help you breakthrough your self-doubts, overcome common challenges, build your self-esteem, and unlock your potential:

IN THIS FREE BONUS GUIDE DISCOVER:

- Building Confidence and Self-Esteem
- The Roots of Low Self-Confidence
- How to Boost your Self-Confidence
- And more...

PLUS BONUS NEW FREE BOOK RELEASES!

SCAN THE QR CODE TO CLAIM YOUR FREE BONUS NOW!

https://bonus.mindsetmastership.com/talk-effectively

WANT A COPY OF MY NEW EBOOK?

Email me:
leonlyonsauthor@gmail.com

"Wherever you go, go with all your heart."
— **Confucius**

MASTERSHIP BOOKS

UK | USA | Canada | Ireland | Australia
India | New Zealand | South Africa | China

Mastership Books is part of the United Arts Publishing House group of
companies based in London, England, UK.
First published by Mastership Books (London, UK), 2023

Cover design by Rich © United Arts Publishing (UK)
Text and internal design by Rich © United Arts Publishing (UK)
Image credits reserved.
Colour separation by Spitting Image Design Studio

Printed and bound in Great Britain
National Publications Association of Britain
London, England, United Kingdom.

Paper design UAP
A723.5

Title: How to Talk Effectively

Design, Bound & Printed:
London, England,
Great Britain.

Change Mindset Books

GET A FREE AUDIOBOOK

EMAIL SUBJECT LINE:

"HOW TO TALK EFFECTIVELY"

TO

leonlyonsauthor@gmail.com

CONTENTS

Introduction   xxi

1. BELIEVE, HEAL, AND GROW   1
   What role does culture play in problems with
   interpersonal contact?   4
   Three main cultural factors can hinder
   effective communication: 4
   Possess Belief in Your Value   5
   Heal   7
   Grow   9
   Key takeaways   13

2. WHY AND HOW WE TELL STORIES   15
   When people tell stories, the culture grow   16
   How to tell stories   20
   Key takeaways   25

3. THE IMPORTANCE OF SPEAKING SKILLS   27
   Key takeaways   31

4. HOW WE INFLUENCE OTHERS   33
   Key takeaways   41

5. HOW TO BUILD RAPPORT AND
   CONNECTION   43
   Let's see how it works in practice.   48
   Key takeaways   51

6. USING IMAGINATION FOR BETTER TALKS   53
   Key takeaways   59

7. HOW TO USE EMOTIVE LANGUAGE   61
   How do we use emotive language?   64
   Key takeaways   66

8. MAKING DIALOGUE PERSONAL   67

   How do you have a stimulating discussion?   67

   Need help with how to start a conversation?   69

   Avoid misunderstandings by taking these
   measures   72

   Be prepared for appropriate moments by
   practicing some polite conversation closers   74

   But what about the introverted and the shy?   75

   Key takeaways   78

9. TYPES OF COMMUNICATION STYLES   79

   What are the types of communication styles?   80

   Passive Communication   80

   Aggressive Communication   81

   Passive-aggressive Communication   82

   Assertiveness   83

   Key takeaways   87

10. TONE OF VOICE   89

   Pitch   90

   Pace   90

   Volume   91

   Timbre   91

   Why is tone of voice so important?   92

   How do you develop a friendly tone of voice?   92

   Having a Friendly Conversation   94

   Key takeaways   96

11. PRACTICE PRONUNCIATION   97

   Pronunciation vs. Accent   98

   Key takeaways   106

12. BODY LANGUAGE   107

   Why is body language significant?   107

   What can a person's body language tell you
   about them?   115

   But how might nonverbal communication be
   enhanced?   116

   Key takeaways   117

13. KNOW YOUR AUDIENCE   119
First determine who you are writing or
speaking to for before beginning   120
Key takeaways   123

14. ORGANIZING THOUGHTS FOR SPEECH   125
Ways to organize your thoughts in the real
world   133
Key takeaways   136

15. PERSUASIVE COMMUNICATION IN
RELATION TO BUSINESS   137
Key takeaways   147

16. PROVOKING DESIRE   149
Key takeaways   153

17. PUBLIC SPEAKING   155
Key takeaways   163

CONCLUSION   165

INTRODUCTION

Every one of us at some point will be required to speak in front of a crowd of strangers. This is a terrifying task that could happen at work or in front of a real audience.

People's opinions of us are heavily affected by how well or poorly we communicate with them. Consequently, many people become very highly strung when they have to give presentations.

Even some of the most successful ones get nervous when they have to speak in front of large groups. When asked, "What makes you nervous?" the most common answer is, "I don't like being watched."

"I don't like having all eyes on me" is another common way to say the same thing or "I don't like being in the spotlight at all."

Almost always, they will only look directly at the audience later in the presentation, well after they've taken the stage. The problem is that avoiding eye contact might seem like a good strategy for overcoming stage fright, but it makes you even more nervous.

The positive news is that you can get over your nerves and give an outstanding performance if you put in the time and energy to prepare and practice.

On the other hand, it would be silly to assume that being afraid of being on stage is the only thing that keeps people from communicating well.

People can't give great speeches for several different reasons, including self-doubt, having trouble connecting with the audience, adopting an unapproachable tone, and a lack of experience. This book was written to help people deal with these problems, which is the good news.

Why is being able to communicate so important?

You can feel more confident if you practice public speaking in front of groups of different sizes. It will help you not only when you are on stage but also when you are in the midst of a business conversation or on a first date.

Speaking engagements are a great way to connect with like-minded people. After you give a presentation, no doubt some individuals will come up to you and start a chat. The process of meeting new people is thus simplified.

Strong public speaking skills can help a person advance in their career because they are a sign of other marketable traits like originality, analytical insight, leadership potential, composure, and expertise. Employers look for all these things in candidates seeking to work for them.

When giving presentations, you will often have to assert your points in a way that makes sense and is convincing. Plus, you can improve your ability to reason by doing research, practicing, and giving speeches, especially if you are given a chance to answer questions from the audience.

Effective communication has a lot of other advantages as well. This brings up the most crucial question: how does one speak in a way that gets results?

The good news is that this book goes into detail about this vital topic. Each step is given a chapter, and each section of the book provides a lot of explanations.

So, do you want to take what follows and apply it to your career? Are you worried about how you will talk to your date in a good way? Do you want to make your case in a more convincing way than anyone else in the room? Because this book was written with you in mind, I implore you to take it easy and read it slowly.

By the time we're done here, I have no doubt that you will have mastered the art of effective communication and go on to do great things.

Dear Reader,

As independent authors, it's often difficult to gather reviews compared with much bigger publishers.

Therefore, please leave a review on the platform where you bought this book.

KINDLE:

LEAVE A REVIEW HERE < click here >

Many thanks,

Author Team

1

BELIEVE, HEAL, AND GROW

Misunderstandings can arise in any setting or between any two people. It's simple to misread or misinterpret another person, which can cause problems during interpersonal, social, and professional interactions. Sometimes disagreements emerge, making it harder to talk to one another.

Suppose you're experiencing distress or difficulties due to communication problems. In this case, it may be good to seek the guidance of a therapist or other mental health expert.

A variety of circumstances can cause interpersonal communication problems. Conflicts among friends or coworkers can be a source of problems if they disagree over matters of opinion. It's common for people to bring up communication difficulties when they go to therapy over relationship problems.

Sometimes, differences in culture or individual experience can lead to friction. As a result of the broad variation in communication practices between cultural groups, the exact words spoken to people from various backgrounds might have dramatically different meanings. Communicators in both the target language and the interlocutor's native tongue may struggle to grasp subtleties and nuances that are obvious to each other, respectively. This might cause misunderstandings, disagreements, and even rudeness where none was intended.

Furthermore, due to cultural differences, an issue regarded as a communication difficulty by someone from one culture may not be found problematic in the least by someone from a different culture.

Disruptions in the flow of information between patient and caregiver can also be caused by the patient's or caregiver's physical or mental condition. It might be frustrating for someone sick or upset to have to explain their symptoms to a new doctor whenever they need help.

Childhood stress, physical and mental health concerns, trauma, misinterpreting another person's comments or motives, failing to grasp another person's point of view, cultural barriers, linguistic disparities, and so on can all hinder effective communication. Also assumptions and generalizations not supported by evidence, refusing to answer questions, hiding information, making hurtful comments, not listening, and so on.

Problems in communicating can be the root cause of conflict in relationships. When problems arise, both partners may be aware of them. Still, they might need to be mindful of their need for better communication regarding these issues. Some couples are convinced that they have good communication skills because they regularly discuss mundane topics, avoiding that tough conversations that could have a lasting effect on their relationship. If a couple is having trouble resolving their differences, taking a closer look at their communication patterns may help.

It's not uncommon for romantic relationships to be negatively impacted by underlying emotional and psychological issues, such as those from one's upbringing, previous romantic relationships, or other parts of life. A relationship might suffer when one partner goes through tough times but doesn't tell the other; this can leave the other person feeling wounded or abandoned. Therapy can resolve communication problems in relationships and families as it investigates underlying causes. Effective communication between partners is a crucial feature of a healthy relationship.

To better handle day-to-day conversations, a person may find it helpful to:

- Make an effort to connect on an emotional level before talking.
- Get your mindset right before attempting to have a conversation on a contentious issue.
- Express your innermost ideas and thoughts clearly.
- Using "I" phrases is an effective way to convey emotion.
- Don't pretend to be someone else when you speak.
- Don't use condescending or insulting language.
- Be a good listener.
- Participate in a public speaking group or debating club (when conversing is what causes difficulty).

What role does culture play in problems with interpersonal contact?

While a common language may help break down language barriers, cultural differences can be just as problematic. Two people who communicate in the same language but from distinct cultural backgrounds may form diverse impressions of a conversation while sharing the same language. The inability to communicate effectively is compounded when one party is not a native speaker of the language used in the conversation.

Three main cultural factors can hinder effective communication:

- Cognitive limitations become apparent in conversations between people with different worldviews and reference points.

- Differences between verbal and nonverbal behavior constitute behavioral restrictions. For example, while some cultures consider it respectful to stare directly into the eyes of a superior when speaking, others may regard such direct eye contact as rude.

- Limitations in emotional expression explain why people show their emotions in different ways. Some people from one culture may show their feelings openly while those from another may keep them hidden behind a wall.

Misunderstandings and conflicts can arise when persons engaging in cross-cultural communications need to account for considering these and other contextual factors.

Having faith in one's abilities is what is meant by "believing in oneself." It involves confidence in one's capabilities to carry out commitments and the ultimate success of one's plans. This indicates that having faith in oneself results from accumulating numerous significant psychological experiences, including those of self-worth, self-confidence, self-trust, self-respect, autonomy, and environmental mastery.

Faith in our abilities activates a cascade of positive psychological responses that boost our success, happiness, and fulfillment. The opposite is also true. When we don't know how to believe in ourselves, we are less inclined to take the initiative to improve our circumstances. This means we increase our chances of failure when we anticipate doing poorly.

Thus, self-confidence can be compared to the key that turns on the ignition and sets the car in motion. Without it, we'd be stuck. Nothing we do seems to help since our goals and values don't align with who we are. Consequently, we either fail to take the necessary actions or undermine ourselves in some way, either consciously or unconsciously.

Possess Belief in Your Value

Recognizing your value is the first and most pivotal step in developing self-confidence. Why bother pursuing your goals if you don't think you deserve them or if you can't convince yourself that you deserve them? However, if you're kind to yourself and treat yourself with the same respect you'd give a friend, you'll find it much easier to have faith in yourself.

Self-compassion and other forms of self-kindness are helpful ways to begin bolstering our sense of value in ourselves. When we have a tough time or make a mistake, we can be kind and encouraging to ourselves. Positive affirmations are a tool for reinforcing the attitudes we want to cultivate toward ourselves.

Accept Yourself for What You Are Good At

Believing in yourself entails recognizing that you already possess the attributes or knowledge necessary to achieve your goals. Now, how does that function, exactly? Making a list of your best traits and abilities is a great place to start, and you can learn their identities through this method.

Next, consider how you may use these strengths to achieve your objectives. Hopefully, you'll rely less on blind faith to trust in yourself after seeing how many positive qualities you possess and how they can be used. Instead, it will be staring you in the face, and you may find yourself saying, "Yes, I am the kind of person who can achieve this objective!"

You will discover that you need more critical strengths to help you achieve your objectives. It would help if you got to work developing those abilities. Nothing in this world equips us with what we need to realize our full potential. So, if there are gaps in your skillset, consider how your existing traits and talents might be used to fill those gaps. Thus, our confidence in ourselves and our ability to accomplish goals increases gradually over time.

Have Faith in Yourself by Fortifying Your Confidence

When we consider trust, we usually conceive it as something we have for other people. But we also trust ourselves (or we don't). The effects of having (or lacking) this faith in oneself are analogous to having (or lacking) trust in other people. As an illustration, when we trust someone, we are open and honest with them. We know we can rely on them, and that they will look out for our best interests.

What does it imply if we don't believe in ourselves? We may be afraid of what we'll do with the truth when we face it. Perhaps we can't rely on our promises to ourselves. On the other hand, we may be reluctant to take positive action for fear of doing more harm than good.

It may sound strange when spoken like this, but many of us struggle to trust our own judgment. For instance, we may have promised ourselves a thousand times that we'll begin exercising, but we never followed through. If we keep telling ourselves we're going to exercise, then how likely are we to do it? It's not going to happen.

Perhaps we've repeatedly told ourselves that our marriage is excellent, even when we know it's declining. Our deception has been monumental. So, how do we know we can rely on our discretion? Because of this, the first step in building confidence is to learn to trust oneself, and we have to become reliable.

Heal

It's human nature to try to steer clear of uncomfortable feelings. Who would want to plunge themselves headfirst into something that will surely hurt? But if you never confront your inner "boogeyman". it will eventually hold you captive. When this happens, people tend to avoid anything that could give them stress and instead occupy themselves with meaningless activities. However, by preventing difficulties that could help you develop and find happiness, you also avoid opportunities that could bring such things.

Running away from your fears will only work for a while. They will eventually explode, no matter how hard you try to bottle them. You can count on it happening when you need to be emotionally stable.

Please consider seeing a therapist if you're struggling with severe anxiety or fear, especially if a phobia has caused it. Here are some tips that have helped many patients overcome their phobias and regain control of their lives:

- Give yourself a few moments to be alone with your fear. Just take a deep breath and reassure yourself that "It's all right. Emotions are like the ocean; they ebb and flow, so even if it hurts now, it won't always. Once your two- or three-minute sitting period is up, immediately engage in a nourishing activity: get in touch with that trusted buddy who's been pining for your call, or throw yourself into something you love to do.

- Record your feelings of gratitude on paper. When you're feeling down, refer to the list. Include in the tally.

- The anxiousness you're feeling is a treasure trove of insight, so tap into it. You might tell say, "Dear Anxiety, I am no longer afraid of you," by penning a letter to it. Asking, "What can I learn from you?"

- Exercise: working out can help you regain concentration (your mind can only fixate on one thing at a time). Exercise is beneficial no matter what form of physical activity you choose—a brisk walk, an intense sweat session at the boxing gym, or a quick 15-minute yoga practice in front of the TV. It will make you feel more grounded and capable.

- Laughing at your darkest concerns will help you deal with them more effectively. What ludicrous worst-case scenarios could occur? For example, if you accept an offer to speak in front of an audience of 500 people? My first boyfriend (girlfriend) will mock me in the audience, and I may wet my pants on the stage. I will be imprisoned for giving the worst speech in history.

- Salute your bravery. One of the most helpful coping mechanisms is treating oneself kindly. What encouraging words would you give a close friend struggling with the fearful thoughts popping into her head? Don't take any risks. Follow your advice: stop caring what other people think and start being your best friend.

Grow

We've put together a few pointers to help you improve your communication abilities. Active listening is a skill you should cultivate. It's possible to get better at listening, even if you already consider yourself an excellent listener.

Checking out the active listening model is a terrific way to identify areas of improvement.

Unlike passive listening, in which one takes in the information and moves on, active listening involves maintaining full attention on the speaker and showing genuine attentiveness to what they have to say. Although there is no definitive model, expect to find some consistent themes throughout your research, such as:

- Tune in when other people are talking.

- You can sense their desire if you ask them open-ended questions.

- Ask questions to get more information on anything you need help understanding. Check your comprehension by paraphrasing and restating what was said.

- Pay attention to how you both feel to meet everyone's requirements.

- Conclude your encounter with a summary to ensure that all parties understand the key points and next steps.

Don't keep your opinions and ideas to yourself; share them.

Make sure you're communicating your demands while also trying to grasp the desires of those around you. If you don't tell anyone, they won't find out. As a leader, you need this talent more than anyone else because your words shape the culture of your team. One way to encourage others to follow your lead is to demonstrate the importance of open and honest communication. They will be more natural to working with others, adjusting their expectations when required, and facing challenges head-on with the belief that they will be overcome.

Please don't assume anything.

It is common to think that you know another person's desires. However, this is a major source of misconceptions and one of the reasons such misunderstandings might lead to conflict. In such a situation, active listening can be a life-saver. The ability to empathize with another person and acknowledging what they are going through is essential for successful communication.

This is significant since words are only sometimes an accurate reflection of intentions. It's typical to try to mask or hide our true feelings, especially when we're in an awkward or difficult circumstance. To avoid misunderstandings and arguments, it is essential to ask questions, pay attention to the replies, and repeat what you believe they intend.

Be mindful of your feelings and thoughts, especially in trying situations like important conversations.

Highly effective communicators have a firm handle on their feelings. When they get angry or overexcited, they know how to rein them in and keep the talk moving along without letting them cause any disruptions. Don't let your negative feelings about something spiral out of control. You should stop what you're doing if your heart rate increases or your face gets hot. Take some time out to relax by yourself.

The ability to recognize and accept responsibility for mistakes is also an essential aspect of self-awareness. Admitting your mistakes and avoiding them in the future may significantly blow your ego. I assure you that you will gain respect and integrity in the eyes of your loved ones and coworkers if you do so.

Never make an accusation when bringing up a problem.

You'll inevitably run into some challenging circumstances. Keep your cool even if the other person has done something you think is very wrong. It's a surefire way to start an argument if you jump right in by blaming the other person for something. After being accused, our first instinct is to defend ourselves, and the outcome of such a discussion is always negative.

Key takeaways

- Emotional expression varies among cultures and individuals. It's not uncommon for people of one culture to display their feelings publicly, whereas those of another culture may choose to keep their emotions under check.
- The best way to develop is to listen attentively, talk about your thoughts and do so deliberately.
- The first step in boosting your self-esteem is realizing your worth.

2

WHY AND HOW WE TELL STORIES

Everyone tells stories. They might be about family, work, and life events. When we can't comprehend out why some situations are the way they are, we sometimes use a story, a folk tale, or a character from a TV show as an example. To make sense of our lives, we make up stories about ourselves.

Storytelling is an integral part of what it signifies to us to be human. In telling a story, we can get information across in a way that sticks with the listener. They help us understand what we are learning and how it fits into the entire perspective. They also help us remember what we have learned. We can learn more about other people's lives through their stories because stories make us feel like we know them. This helps us understand what they went through, learn from their experiences, and use them in our lives.

It's easy to remember stories, and they help us remember names, dates, places, and events long after we've forgotten them. The magic of a good tale is that it stays with you long after you've forgotten the details. Someone might think of your company as the story's setting. In a world where a great deal of things are trying to get our attention, telling a story that connects with your audience emotionally may significantly affect how they see your brand.

The best way to understand life is through someone's story. The majority of our time is spent telling different stories: everything from online status updates and in-person chats to phone calls and coffee shop meetings is a story, for the most part. When we tell our partners about our day at work, that's a story. When our kids tell us about their day at school, that's another story. When we talk about what we learned from the news, that's also a story.

Social media sites like Twitter, Instagram, Facebook, and TikTok make it effortless than ever for everyone to share their stories. Experts used to be the go-to sources for marketing content. Still, it's all about the customer and their opinions and experiences. People will trust your brand more if they hear stories from others who have used it. So, start telling people about your successes.

When people tell stories, the culture grow

A solid business culture can only be built on the backs of dedicated employees, encouraging them to share their personal stories. Remind your employees often of why the organization exists, who it has helped, and the fantastic things it has done along the way. These stories will be interesting to everyone who knows your team. When done right, corporate storytelling can boost productivity and encourage people to work as a team.

Stories can easily change how people feel.

Most people get emotional when they see the John Lewis Christmas commercial. Why? Because it is a sad story meant to make us feel something. True to form, this is what stories do. Human interest stories touch you personally, making it more likely that you act on what they are pitching.

Your feelings and points of view come through in the way you speak and write. Stories can make people feel things, but they also show who the person telling the story is. Any effective leader will tell you how necessary it is to have a clear, focused vision for where you want to take your team. So, be honest and proud when you tell your story.

Don't be afraid to say to people the dirty truth.

People want the truth; nothing is more moving than a story based on actual events. It will help your company's reputation, get the word out about your business, and encourage other people to join you. Let the stories start!

Everyone has an exciting story; the world is full of them.

If something is making you feel heavy and you need to get rid of it, you can find relief by talking about it. Putting yourself out there requires courage by telling a personal story. You let go of your burden and accept your dark side. With this method, better health can be achieved.

Most of us are afraid of speaking in the presence of others.

We also dislike showing people who we truly are. Why not do both at once? Going on stage and talking about your life is a special way to feel better about yourself. You can show your weaknesses to different people without fear. Feel free to talk about what you think and feel. More people will positively respond if you add personality to your message. Try to give it all you've got.

Everyone has their own way of expressing themselves.

The goal is to find your voice, personality, and poetry. Even at your weakest, you'll find a voice that is uniquely yours that can fit any situation. When you take the stage, you use more than just your voice. Like a dancer, you must be present in your body, fully awake and aware of your movements; but you will not be self-conscious. To add meaning to your story, connect with your audience and portray a spectrum of emotions.

After telling the world about your experience and finding people who can see you, you will be in harmony with yourself and others. Simply put, you are no longer secretive or keeping information inside. You've brought your darkness into the light; so now your spirit, body, and mind are all in sync. The key to happiness is alignment.

When you finally tell your story, you'll have something solid to "anchor" your life. After sharing your story and gaining perspective and peace, it will be much easier to let go of things or people making you feel bad. Finding a group of people captivated by the same things as you is great for maintaining a good mood. People who share your beliefs will be drawn to you after hearing your story because they see a kindred spirit in you. You have honed your values and vision for the future by carefully writing and telling your account, allowing you to look for a social neighborhood that fits you best.

Barriers can be broken by telling a story.

We are sometimes surprised at how a story ends. We don't question or fight against it because it doesn't make sense or follow a pattern. We listen to it, think about it, and feel it in our bodies. We depend more upon our creative than our analytical skills.

A good story can be a source of inspiration.

A lot of us have to work to pay attention to a presentation that is highly analytical and logical. We do it the same way we did our math and physics homework in high school: methodically and persistently. On the other hand, a story can keep hold our attention the whole time. When we go to new places and learn to look at things we already know in a new way, we grow as people.

In short, a good story can change the way you see things. People, their goals, and our understanding of how things work can all be "framed" by the stories we hear.

The best method to leave a lasting impression is through storytelling.

People will remember the stories from a speech long after they have forgotten the main points. Anecdotes that are well-chosen can help the audience remember the most important parts of the address.

Stories get us to feel things.

When we get into a book, we start to feel like one of the characters and go through the same experiences. The strength of our emotions makes them stronger. When we read a story, we sometimes feel all emotions: happiness, sadness, relief, and laughter.

How to tell stories

Great leaders use stories to inspire their followers, and great writers use them to create works of literature that will last forever. If you are starting with storytelling, here are some tips to help you build your stories and keep your audience interested:

Get a clear statement of your main point.

The best stories have a clear lesson or moral shown to the reader bit by bit. When writing a story, knowing where you're going is essential. If the story has a moral, you should point the reader or listener in that direction. When telling a funny story, it's common to build up to a twist that makes everyone laugh out loud.

Build up the tension and drama until the climax when telling a gripping story.

No matter what genre you're composing or telling aloud, it would help to have a firm grasp of the story's main idea or plot point.

Accept and welcome differences of opinion.

You can't tell a good story without some tension. Good storytellers put their main characters through hell by putting them in dangerous situations. If the main characters are going to reach their goals, the audience has to care about them and want them to do well. It's not only okay but often necessary to be hard on your main characters. To get better at telling stories, you must learn to love conflict and drama, which makes stories all the more interesting.

Use an easy-to-understand format.

A story needs an introduction, a middle, and an end, but there are many ways to combine these parts. In more detail, a well-told story starts with a turning point, builds up to a climax, and ends on a satisfying note. If you want to study more about these ideas and other ways to tell stories, you can find many books and articles online. Story structure can be better understood by reading and watching stories by great storytellers, plotting out one's reports on paper, and then analyzing their form and function.

Check out what you remember of your past.

You can always get story ideas from your own life, whether or not you're telling a true story. Think about the critical events in your life and how you can utilize them.

Learn how to win over your listeners.

An essential part of being a compelling storyteller is being able to strike a chord with your listeners, but how you achieve that depends heavily upon your delivery. If you're giving a public reading of a short story, try looking up from the page every so often at the people in the room. When you record a narrative podcast, it's essential that your voice be expressive and you show emotion through your tone. Regardless of your story, think about who you're telling it to.

Learn how to tell stories from the best. There is no craftier way to learn how to tell a story than to listen to and watch the storytellers you like. We all know people who are great at speaking and telling stories. You've met a lot of great storytellers in your life no doubt. It could be family members who like to tell stories about their youth at the dinner table or members of your local government who are very articulate. Listen to great storytellers and write down what they do to get better at telling stories. How do they make stories that are interesting to read?

Condense what happens in your story.

When telling a true story, it might take effort to decide which parts to highlight. Some people tend to go into too much detail, which only serves to bore the reader and dilutes the story's main point. Choose a beginning and an ending for your story, then use bullet points to describe what happens in the middle. Trust that your readers can follow the story as it continues, and don't tire them with too much explanation.

Use what you've learned in the real world.

The best stories teach lessons by showing how they work in real life. Using accounts from your own life to prove your point will make you seem more real and exciting. Use funny stories, problems you've solved, or lessons you've learned.

Even though stories from real life can help you make your point, you shouldn't feel bad if you're more comfortable dwelling in the world of fiction. To tell a story with more imagination, you still need to maintain a clear structure and tell it convincingly.

Remember to write down your story ideas.

Keep a journal for story ideas as they come to you. Always keep one with you to ensure you will never forget a great idea. If you write anything down, even a single sentence, it might help you develop an idea for a future story.

Include your story's lesson in the plot.

One thing that makes a story suitable is that it has a message behind it. Consider the lesson your story can teach, whether you're giving a speech or trying to inspire people. If you need help finding a connection, think of an experience you've had that fits the bill, or look at your idea diary.

For example, if you want your team to work hard to meet a deadline, you could tell them a story about how someone overcame a particular problem. One way to teach this lesson is to talk about a time when the group worked together to solve a problem.

Put others' needs ahead of your own.

No one likes it when someone talks about how great they are. Even though it's good to use real-life examples, the main character of your stories shouldn't be you.

In stories where you play a crucial role, you might learn something from an older character or make a rookie mistake. In this way, your audience will feel more connected to you and invested in your story. You won't come across as arrogant or boastful. It would help if you gave some thought to how you start and how you end. The listener will be interested in what comes next if the beginning is interesting. Start on the right foot by asking a thought-provoking question, telling a funny joke, or explaining what you want to say. As you wrap up your story, it's essential to go back to the beginning and explain how you got to where you are now.

Include interesting details.

A good story needs vivid information that makes the audience part of the action. Be descriptive, but give them only a little tantalizing information.

Key takeaways

- A compelling story is the most effective means of making an enduring impression.
- Stories have the power to shape communities and alter how people feel.
- The best stories have engaging characters, a straightforward structure, and an implicit moral.

3

THE IMPORTANCE OF SPEAKING SKILLS

Why is speaking ability important? Even though a picture is supposed to be worth a thousand words, if the image is hazy or challenging, it is more likely that words will be necessary. After all, talking to one another is the most effective method of communication. As a consequence, speech is an essential component of the process.

Some links may be made between the four elements of language proficiency: listening, reading, and writing. A well-rounded communicator will be skilled in all communication aspects. Still, strong public speaking abilities will give the speaker many tangible rewards. Because they can meaningfully blend words to express their thoughts, beliefs, and feelings, the speaker enjoys the following substantial benefits as a result of this ability:

The capacity to guide, persuade, and inform

Among others, business executives, educators, military commanders, lawyers, and politicians aim to improve their speaking abilities to the point where they become master communicators. A speaker can capture an audience's attention by speaking clearly and firmly, giving them the prime opportunity to communicate their point. A wise speaker captures and then maintains the audience's engagement, using carefully chosen words in a presentation that is effective and easily understood.

The capacity to stand out from the competition

Speaking abilities are frequently considered to be standard abilities. Think again. It takes a unique talent to communicate clearly in front of people. Many people are utterly frightened of speaking in front of a group. In contrast, others struggle to organize their thoughts into complete sentences and then convincingly deliver them. The unfortunate reality is that there are not many people alive today who possess the same level of oratory ability as John F. Kennedy or Winston Churchill. The good news is that a speaker who develops their abilities through consistent effort and hard work can stand out.

Ability to gain indirectly

One's ability to negotiate can be improved by having strong language abilities. Self-assurance is raised. Speaking in front of ever-larger crowds leads to an increase in comfort. Over time, a speaker may develop a reputation for speaking well, lending them some credibility.

Improving one's career

Employers have always valued the ability to communicate effectively. Because it is and will continue to be an essential skill, putting in the effort to develop it to its full potential is highly worthwhile.

Personal fulfilment

When delivering a presentation that connects with an appreciative audience, speakers frequently experience a profound degree of fulfillment that is uncommon in other types of communication. When a crowd shows their outward admiration for a speaker, the familiar apprehension might give way to sentiments of success and joy. It's compensation for all the effort and planning that goes into honing your skills.

Persuasive speaking is one of the goal, whether it is to persuade your manager to support your proposal, your team to put in more effort, or your spouse to watch your favorite movie. All these situations call for effective speaking. Being able to influence others' opinions is the entire point of speaking skills, i.e., to control them to act in line with your objectives.

When you're in a professional context, having the ability to communicate well will help you stand out from every other person and establish you as a valued resource for your organization. Naturally, this offers you an advantage over the other people in your workplace.

Effective communicators are given particular respect in an organization, as they are frequently requested to represent the company in various settings. They seal transactions with essential customers, meet with significant clients, and build a reputation for providing excellent customer service.

For example, you could send your best salesperson to meet with a potential new customer. You would not put in a newcomer but someone with experience. In nearly all cases, the person who is your best speaker is your best salesperson.

Regarding promotions and bonuses, speakers are given preference over other employees. Many companies place a significant emphasis on the education of their workforce; they are the ones who are ready to take on positions of authority because of their preparation.

Speaking ability is fundamental. Since they have written multiple drafts of each speech, influential speakers are also effective writers. Additionally, effective communicators are those who can relate to others. They become approachable and genuine as a result, and people gravitate toward them frequently for support and guidance. They are also readers since reading broadens one's vocabulary and cultivates the style of using appropriate words in various contexts. So, honing your speaking abilities helps to improve your writing, listening, and reading skills.

Key takeaways

- Good speeches need research; and becoming an expert in effective communication signals subject-matter expertise. A good speaker is therefore regarded as a leader and an influencer.
- Effective speaking abilities are required for success and influence.
- Making a real connection with the audience makes you feel accomplished. Self-esteem is significantly increased by listening to the applause of the audience. For all the effort a speaker puts in, being appreciated by the audience is like getting a gift.
- Speaking abilities are crucial for career success, but they are relevant to more than just one's goals in terms of a career. Speaking skills can improve a person's personal life and lead to overall development

4

HOW WE INFLUENCE OTHERS

We often think that a person's influence comes from self-confidence, intelligence, and charisma. It could come with a high position or more money as you age. This skill is something we all have, and most of us don't use it to its fullest extent because we think being influential is something we're born with.

Influence skills don't just come out of nowhere; it's a skill that needs to be practiced and worked on. The people we look up to are showing us the way with a tried-and-true method.

Make sure you can be counted on.

People often think that influence can come and go whenever they want. It's important to look out for others' best interests and earn their trust. Building trust and showing genuine interest are critical first steps if you want to get them to do something. It would be best to indicate that you are honest and helping others is your top priority. To win over your audience, you must present yourself honestly.

People will remember you best if you are yourself and not a copy of someone else's idea of what it means to be authentic.

Learning how to embrace and accept your unique point of view on a subject is important. Most influential people on social media got where they are because they filled a void in the market or came up with a novel solution to a widespread problem. People naturally gravitate to people who are the same in public and private. We dislike inconsistencies because we like things to stay the same. When someone says they are one thing but act in a contradictor way, it's a red flag that they are either confused or not trustworthy, making them fake. With either of these combinations, you will likely have a poor effect on other people.

Show up and make a connection.

Try listening more and talking less if you want to be in the moment. If you listen carefully, you'll be able to tell what makes the other person upset. When you figure out what feelings are behind their decisions, you can show that you have really listened to them and taken them seriously. They will probably resist your efforts if you seem uninterested, dishonest, or focused on yourself.

Solicit clarification.

Compared to other ways of talking, asking questions is the most convincing approach. The more questions you ask, the better the conversation goes. Before effectively encouraging someone, you need to know what is most important to them. Is their goal to change the world, earn their peers' respect, or advance in their careers? What do they think is most important? What are they going through in their lives?

Give them a series of open-ended questions and then ask them to explain their answers over and over. The real answer will never come from the first question, so dig deeper. It would be best if you got to the bottom of why they act as they do. If you can't motivate someone, you need to know what prompts them.

Check your ideas and think about what people say about them.

As a first rule, you shouldn't try to prove the other person wrong. They will get angry whenever you do something to hurt them, and you will lose. If any of their suspicions are true, you should talk about it. No one is better than you at pointing out your flaws. You'll win their trust and establish credibility by addressing their concerns before they object.

Learn your genre well.

Most of the time, people are more likely to follow those in charge, even if they do not respect them. Demonstrating your expertise in the field your audience engages in is the surest route to getting them to do what you desire. Read as much as possible about the topic, then try to find ways to use what you've learned. Opinions are fair game for debate. But experts have facts, and arguing with them is not a good idea.

Find the good in people.

People are easier to get along with when you catch them doing nice things. Don't waste time worrying about everything that went right; instead, focus on what didn't. Take note of the small stuff your coworkers, subordinates, and bosses do that make work more productive and enjoyable. Remember to give perks when due whenever you encounter a deed well done. Taking an interest in other people's accomplishments is a great way to establish the professional and personal rapport you're hoping to achieve. Complimenting someone is a simple way to improve their day.

Instead of saying you're sorry, show you care.

It's easy to feel like you always need to prove yourself. If you don't trust yourself and care more about what other people think, it's important to be right. Ego-feeding happens when other people agree with what you believe (i.e., when you are proven "right").

But when we try to prove that we are right, we sometimes hurt other people and worsen things. It's far more challenging to get someone to do what we want when we harm them by being mean.

The way to stop being mean to others is to put empathy ahead of being right. You can be polite and firm in what you believe in simultaneously. Many people think they need outside confirmation of how they feel inside. You might get upset if other people don't see the situation as you do, but in the end, what matters is what you know.

It's unnecessary to wait for your dining partners to concur that the restaurant's cuisine was terrible before leaving if you and they end up feeling ill after eating there. The only proof you need is that you've had food poisoning yourself. Trying to prove a point is a waste of time; and if you were rude while trying to prove that you got food poisoning, you are letting yourself down.

Find out what a person needs to think, feel, and work with others.

The best course of action to get people to follow what you want them to do is to appeal to their needs: logical, emotional, and cooperative. The apparent need comes from good reasoning and good teaching, and if the information that meets their emotional needs significantly impacts them. The cooperative stance is knowing how much help different people need and then giving it to them accordingly.

Realizing that everyone has slightly different needs is the key to using this method well. Some people will give more weight to strong emotional arguments than logical ones. For others, the chance to work together will be more important than any emotional connection. If you know your target market well, you'll be able to give them exactly what they want, making it more likely to have good effect. You need to know more about the people you are trying to persuade to do so.

Understand Your Lane.

The key to persuading others to do what you want is to focus on what's within your purview, area of influence or competence and delegate the rest. People used to be praised for being able to "do it all," but those days are long gone.

Brands do well in the marketplace when they know what their customers want and then give it to them. When someone focuses on their strengths and uses them to help others, they are more effective. It's great that this works so well.

Focusing on what other people have done instead of what you have done makes it impossible to have a positive effect on those around you.

Make an effort to be amenable.

Being influential helps you seem friendly and easy to talk to. People who are sure of themselves are more likely to be followed by others. You shouldn't, however, talk down to anyone. Instead of treating people like younger siblings, be friends with them. When you are humble about your skills, people like you less.

Be sure to smile. People are drawn to friendly people, which shows that you are pleasant and trustworthy.

Make inquiries.

Have conversations that matter with other people. If you care about them, they will respond in a good way. Another easy way to break the ice and start talking to someone is to ask for a pencil or offer to help with anything they need.

Set up a timetable. Make a group trip happen, like a hike or a trip to a show, and get people to join in. This will clearly show that you respect them and are interested, helping you make friends with them.

Influence people with your genuine interest.

Starting a conversation with someone is a proven way to establish a favorable first impression. Their advice should be taken seriously. In fact, good listening skills are one of the most advantageous methods of getting to know someone. To get someone's attention, you should ask them questions that make them think. Give answers that show you have thought about the subject. For example, don't tell a joke when someone is talking about how serious their illness is. If you answer correctly, you can build trust and strengthen the relationship.

Talk about what other people find interesting.

Asking people about the things that interest them is one of the ideal ways to show that you care. It's also a great way to start a conversation with someone to learn more about them, which is necessary when making any connection. When the conversation turns to something they're interested in, you can get anyone to open up. If you find out that someone reads a lot, ask them about the best book they've read in the last few months. Find out how they got into rock climbing and if they'd be willing to take you out on a climb sometime. Don't take over the conversation by talking about yourself and what you like. Remember that your goal is to get them to pay attention. Keep the subject the same if they are genuinely interested in your recent skydiving trip.

Be friendly and easy to talk to.

If you want someone to see things your way, start by being nice. Don't be overbearing or demanding. Just ask them yes/no questions. This will get them on board right away. Use a public announcement like, "Hey, I'm going to get some groceries at the store. If you could come with me, that would be great."

Recognize that the points of view of those who disagree with you are valid.

Focus on the awareness of the other person's point of view. Why do they do what they do? When you respect others' beliefs, they will do the same for you and yours. If you are aware of why people think the way they do, even if you clash with them, it gives the impression that you're willing to consider other points of view.

Key takeaways

- Influence is a learned skill, not a gift you are born with.
- Be easy to get along with, show empathy, and ask questions; these are ways to work toward building your influence.
- The principal way to convince people to follow what you want them to do is to prove you are an expert in an area in which they should be interested.

5

HOW TO BUILD RAPPORT AND CONNECTION

Establishing a good rapport is necessary to keep effective communication in process. When was the last conversation you had that left you feeling you had immediately let your guard down? No doubt it was uncomplicated and straightforward. You may have sensed an instant connection or chemistry between you, probably because you two got along instantly and could connect. On the other hand, it takes some time to reach a degree of familiarity that is comfortable with most people. Building rapport in a professional environment requires the same level of intention and effort as in any other.

Based on your job, you may be required to put a lot of effort into getting along with people and maintaining good relationships. This chapter will discuss what it means to make a connection with others. There will be a detailed step-by-step plan for getting in touch with anyone quickly and easily.

First, let's grasp the meaning of the term "rapport" so we can use it appropriately. The term describes a connection that may be amicable and harmonious. The fact that both parties are on the same page and can understand what each other is saying - while empathizing with what each other - helps the conversation run smoothly. When you have a positive relationship with another person, there is the expectation that the two of you are collaborating in some way to achieve a goal for your mutual benefit. It will be easier for you to speak with that individual with less chance of a misunderstanding.

Before a link can be judged as rapport, several preconditions must be satisfied first.

These include coordination, awareness of one another, and good coordination. the dynamic structure of rapport is based on the intriguing nonverbal character of these components.

A few straightforward steps can go further toward improving the quality of your social connections. First impressions are shaped by an accumulation of numerous seemingly insignificant activities. It could be demonstrated with a firm handshake and a kind grin. The solution could be as simple as attempting to create eye contact and using the person's name more often. Your initial impression will set the tone for the talk; with time, trust and comprehension will grow between you. Always remember how you want to appear to the person you are encountering for the first time.

Was there a recent time when you participated in a conversation where you felt cut off before completing what you were saying? Or, during a conversation, did one person continued on, cutting the other person off. It's not a very enjoyable experience, as it leaves a bad taste in one's mouths when they first meet. You must tune in and pay close attention. Be attentive to what is being said and interact with the person speaking. You must be capable of paying close attention to what people say if you want to contribute something insightful.

Everyone has had the experience of conversing with only themselves at some point, and such one-sided interactions lead to tenuous connections. Therefore, asking fascinating and pertinent questions is of the utmost importance. Find out which of the many questions you have about this individual are essential. What exactly are you curious about? What kinds of inquiries are most effective in establishing a strong foundation for a connection? What are the specifics of your plan? How may you show the other person that you care?

Following this, you will be able to construct questions that will assist you in achieving the goals you have set for the talk. Participate actively in the discussion and focus on fully comprehending their responses rather than planning your own line of inquiry.

Your body language reveals a lot about you. Using appropriate nonverbal clues is crucial to connecting with others, which includes posture, eye contact, facial emotions, and an awareness of distractions. Not paying attention in a conversation can be seen when one person keeps glancing down at their phone or away. A lack of regular eye contact might give the impression that the other person needs to listen or be more interested in the conversation.

It isn't be fair to judge a book by its cover. Assumptions about commonalities between people are often formed quickly after only one or two sentences have been exchanged during introductions. However, when you get to know someone better, you discover that you have much in common.

When two people come to understand and respect one another, they form the foundation for a good, long-lasting relationship. Establishing rapport requires demonstrating empathy and respect. This stage is a fundamental aspect of threading your interactions with other people. Demonstrate your concern by taking the initiative to put yourself in the other person's shoes. Above and beyond empathy, respect must be the guiding principle of your leadership. Take the Golden Rule to heart and act toward others the way you want them to treat you. If you accomplish this, you'll be in a stronger position to forge connections with other people.

There are several contexts in which rapport is crucial. I will now go over three of the most compelling arguments for putting effort into fostering relationships.

Trust is formed in this way

Maintaining trust between two people over time is difficult. There can be no deep and lasting connection without it. Relationships at the workplace are no different from personal ones in this regard. If you want to move up in the management ranks, your boss must have confidence in you, for instance. They have to believe that you can carry out your duties competently. They must know that you are dedicated to growing as a leader. So, too, it goes in terms of one's interpersonal interactions. Establishing trust is essential to every new friendship. Friendship is built on trust, which is necessary for opening up.

Efficiency in business operations might be boosted as a result

Your ability to network is crucial, no matter what field you're in. Plus, a good working relationship might boost productivity. To illustrate, consider those who work in sales.

It has been shown that a salesperson's efforts pay off better when they spend more time getting to know their customers. Having strong interpersonal skills can make or break your success in the sales workplace.

Your bonds with others will be strengthened as a result

According to scientific research, social contacts are essential for health, pleasure, and a longer lifespan. But it's impossible to have meaningful relationships without some chemistry. In addition, neglecting your emotional well-being might have adverse effects on your physical health. Researchers have found that people with fewer social ties are more likely to get heart disease, diabetes, and suffer from high blood pressure. Suicide, sadness, and anxiety are just some mental health issues that can spike. Poor social and emotional health also makes you more likely to engender health problems. Stress, inflammation, and high blood sugar (hyperglycemia) can all be made worse by feeling alone.

- So, you've decided to start putting effort into your connections. However, getting started could take a lot of work. To facilitate communication and friendship, we have included nine sample phrases:
- In your experience, what advice has proved to be the most helpful?
- Please tell me a little secret that few people know about yourself.
- What makes you feel the most accomplished?
- Please tell me a little secret that few people know about yourself.

- Why would you want that particular superpower if you could have any?
- Which book do you find yourself rereading the most?
- If you could sum up your day in one sentence, how would you describe it?
- Tell me about a recent insight that has enriched your life.
- Where do you hope tomorrow's innovations will take you and your workplace?
- What are your expectations?

Let's see how it works in practice.

Deborah considers Steph to be an inspiration. Deborah has been working for her company for a while but has yet to move up or look for other jobs. She wants a new challenge but is still determining how to handle it professionally. During their conversation over coffee, Steph asks, "What's the best advice you've ever received?"

And then there's John. John and Hannah have been in touch as of late. He found out that Hannah now lives in a different city. Hannah, too, has decided to switch gears and pursue a new career path. John has noticed that Hannah is eager to learn, even though she is still getting to know people. John asks, "What's one book you would read over and over again?" when discussing current reading material.

We'll wrap up by considering Leroy. In this group, Leroy takes on the role of leader. He is the new boss because he was brought in from outside the company and is holding individual sessions with each of his subordinates. Your goal is to leave a favorable impression on Leroy. On the other hand, you're curious about him, his leadership philosophy, and what you may expect from him. You ask, "What's one difficulty in our work that you wish you could address tomorrow?" when discussing his plans for the team.

If you're a manager or supervisor, you might be on the lookout for strategies that foster team chemistry. Since having a positive rapport with others is imperative to the success of any business, it's vital to work on building rapport. It dramatically affects how people feel in the company. The quality of interactions between coworkers and management dramatically determines how long employees stay with a company, how happy they are, and how engaged in their work they are.

Here are some strategies to help your staff become more friendly with one another:

Employees should be encouraged to socialize in a less formal situation, such as over a cup of coffee.

These brief interactions between two workers are not complicated in any way, and they are only sometimes associated with the place of employment. Motivate your workers to make personal and professional connections with one another.

Invest financial resources in enhancing the working environment of your staff.

Does your organization offer an opportunity for the employees to socialize, in-person or virtually, with one another? Does your company participate in volunteer initiatives, team-building exercises, or other forms of clubs and organizations? In order to plan activities hosted by the company that will serve as discussion starters and encourages bonding between employees, what strategies are you utilizing to organize these events?

Insist that the development of meaningful connections with other people be the focus of any opportunity for career progression.

Establish avenues for ongoing education that revolve around developing techniques to strengthen personal and professional relationships.

Make it easier for people to access mentoring programs.

When it comes to helping your staff improve their communication skills, a little individualized coaching goes a long way toward ensuring that they do well. In addition, you must get plenty of experience practicing clear and effective communication.

Key takeaways

- Small talk is the foundation of any good relationship. You can start talking almost right away, which could lead to a deep conversation full of open-ended questions that help people get to know each other better.
- Interpersonal skills are essential for making and keeping connections with other people. People need to be aware of how they feel. As such, they should listen carefully and ask good questions to find out more. The two people involved also need to work on building trust with each other.
- It's never too soon to begin establishing rapport.

6

USING IMAGINATION FOR BETTER TALKS

Maintaining attention for an extended period of time during a presentation is a challenge for many. Without audience participation, people will fidget with their phones, chat with coworkers, and otherwise tune out. Because of your growing concern, you may rush through your presentation if you notice that your audience would rather be doing something else.

To keep the attention of a sizable crowd, the presentation must have the energy and focus of a candid discussion between you and those watching. That way, they can visualize what you're talking about and take away some helpful information while having fun.

Imagine yourself in the shoes of your target demographic when planning. If you want to give an excellent presentation, keep these things in mind:

- How do I determine the most exciting aspects of my subject?
- In what way advanced is my target audience? What skill level should I aim for?

- Who among the listeners is most likely to be bored?
- How can I best ensure that they absorb and comprehend the material?
- How many people are expected to show up?

You can answer these questions by learning as much as possible about the event or conference, the other speakers, and the attendees by getting in touch with the event organizers.

Asking and answering questions about your target demographic will get you thinking about what most likely should appeal to them. Keep in mind that you want to give the impression that careful consideration was given to the interests of the people viewing your presentation.

Create a simple to follow journal

It is always best to prioritize clarity and simplicity while crafting your presentation's framework. To leave your audience with a clear takeaway message, first introduce the main ideas and objectives, then provide more details on each point you've made before lastly drawing the logical conclusions. As if telling a long story in chapters, you want the transitions between sections to be seamless.

Elicit instant participation from the audience

Your listeners will be in various emotional states as they enter your presentation. Try employing a quick icebreaker to energize them so they stay in the presentation mindset.

For instance, you may have the audience stand up and introduce themselves to others sitting nearby, or you could have them write down two or three questions they have on the topic that you'll be covering. Using an icebreaker as the first portion of your discussion signals to the audience that they will be expected to participate.

Incorporate audience Q&A into your presentation

After only ten to fifteen minutes into your presentation, the interest of your audience will have faded entirely. Getting them interested again requires a break from the presentation to engage with the audience. Take questions from the audience during your talk. Any questions or doubts the audience may be dispelled.

Find natural breaks in your material. If you feel awkward pausing mid-presentation to answer questions, let your audience know you'll be doing so at the end. Then they can come up with questions in advance.

You may engage your audience and get them thinking by peppering your presentation with rhetorical questions to smoothly transition from one area to the next.

Create more of an impact by narrating a tale

Stories have played a significant role in human culture since our earliest ancestors. Telling a story is an excellent method to engage listeners, paint a mental image in their minds, and make them interested in what you have to say. This holds no matter what your educational or occupational history is.

Judging from the vast majority of presentations, only some people realize that anecdotes are far more exciting and memorable than dry lists of data (particularly academic ones).

When you begin delivering your narrative, people's attention is instantly drawn to you because they can't wait to hear what happens next. One standard plot device is to describe the current situation before showing the audience a better way to achieve the goal.

Consider the entire presentation as one cohesive story. As discussed, make sure there is a beginning, middle, and end. Conflict can be introduced and a firm resolution provided to cement your messages further.

Make jokes (where appropriate)

Some of the best speeches and presentations contain a lot of humor. Regardless of the topic, an outstanding orator will use their charisma, sense of humor, and command of the language to make their arguments and captivate their audience.

Obama's joke about the government's Iron Man building was a masterclass in using humor to connect with his audience.

Another time is when Morgan Spurlock was selling the naming rights to his TED talk (which he mentioned at the conclusion and when he announced the title) to the highest bidder. He used witty asides throughout the presentation that complemented his main argument.

Like these luminaries, you can also mak

e jokes about the material or find another way to inject humor into the discussion. Your listeners will be far more interested in what you have to say and more likely to remember it.

Find a way to connect with the listeners.

Draw parallels to something most people have experienced. By keeping things straightforward, you'll not only assist your listeners in grasping the topic at hand by giving them a concrete image to work with, but they'll also feel more connected to you.

You're just average folks with comparable backgrounds, playing various roles for the time being.

Don't forget to look your audience in the eyes at all times

One of the most effective methods of engaging an audience is making direct eye contact. Making direct, sustained eye contact with the person you are addressing adds a great deal of personalization to your words and increases their impact. The presenter risks coming across as uneasy and weak by not making eye contact.

Maintaining eye contact with your audience, no matter how big or tiny is crucial. Give your entire presentation to the individual evaluating your work, and keep eye contact with those you know. Remember that the key to a successful presentation is getting the audience involved.

When you're anxious, making and keeping eye contact is a significant challenge. Keep in mind that making eye contact is preferable to none, and do all you can to boost your self-assurance gradually.

If you have access to them, real-world props are recommended

The presentation can be something other than a product demonstration if you use props. this is a terrific strategy to get your audience to envision mentally what you're describing. Suppose you have a prop handy during your presentation. You can pull it out at crucial moments to illustrate your point or clarify something for the audience.

This is precisely what Kenny Nguyen achieves in his TEDx talk titled, "The Art of Saying No." He says that you need both the "sword of yes" and the "shield of no." He grabs a sword and shields off the table to illustrate his points, as one would expect.

An excellent case is when Jill Bolte Taylor, who suffered a stroke, brings a real human brain on stage in her TED talk to illustrate what occurred to her. With this display, she moved the audience and left them in amazement.

Make use of figurative language and other literary devices

The language you employ significantly impacts how you connect. Communicate with your target audience by speaking their language.

Depending upon the topic at hand and the level of expertise of the listeners, you should avoid using language that is either too professional or casual, too technical or simplistic. Although it may be difficult, presenting at the proper level will significantly increase audience participation.

Key takeaways

- Engaging your listeners is crucial if you want to make an impression. Your audience should feel drawn in by your presentation, and their interest, attention, and comprehension should be piqued throughout it.
- Planning your presentation with language and ideas that your audience can grasp is of the utmost importance. You should also leave enough time for people to ask questions and share their thoughts. How you make your presentation should establish rapport with your listeners.
- To ensure that the entire audience receives favorable messages about you and your topic, use eye contact, body language, spoken words, and energy.

7

HOW TO USE EMOTIVE LANGUAGE

"Emotive language" evokes strong feelings in the mind of the public. The words you choose to convey your feelings must be carefully crafted to have the most impact on your audience. Whether speaking to an audience or writing to them, using emotive language is the best method to get their attention.

Expressive language is another term for emotive language. The employment of specific language prompts emotional responses from the audience. The meaning of what we write and say profoundly affects the words we choose. Depending upon the choice of words, the reception from the audience will take many forms.

One definition of "emotive language" is any form of verbal communication that conveys an emotional state. This vocabulary is widely used in many types of stories and works of literature and connects the writer to their audience. Readers should keep in mind language revisions as a wide range of words can express the same feeling – a emotive language helps evoke emotions.

Emotive language keeps your emotions in check

The use of emotive language tools in talks is supported by scientific research as an effective method for resolving emotional turmoil, issues, and traumas. Recording your feelings regularly, even in response to mundane events, can result in profound personal development. Without a doubt, writing in a personal journal will bring up many uncomfortable emotions and feelings. Still, it can be a tremendously effective tool for personal growth.

Emotive language paints a vivid picture of our past events

It has been noticed that the emotional fallout from traumatic events might lead to dissociation. This implies that our brains, to protect us from emotional pain, numb us. As a result, we don't feel those abandoned feelings until they bubble up to the surface and cause difficulty. In this case, the emotive mode of communication can be a lifesaver by bringing buried emotions to the surface, where they can be handled in a healthy way.

Emotive language increases the healing process

Emotional conversations make the audience *feel* something about the story. This is quite therapeutic since it allows the communicator to hear their voice, validating their experience and perhaps helping them move past it. This kind of communication is crucial since it facilitates conversations between the communicator and the audience. In this way, the expressive mode of conversing enables recovery.

Let's briefly talk about connotation.

What a language suggests is what is meant by connotation. Over and above what may be understood at face value, this is the intended symbolic meaning. Different words have different connotations; therefore, to elicit a particular response from your audience, you must choose your words carefully.

An easy way to grasp this idea is by associating colors with words. The color red evokes strong emotions in everyone. White symbolizes innocence while black represents death. It is common for writers and speakers to use connotation games to steer the focus of their audience away from a particular topic or create a new one.

You should now proceed to attempt an analysis of emotive language and its meanings, given your newfound familiarity with the concept. As a starting point, think about the desired reaction from the listeners' emotional centers. After that, you must figure out how the response fits into the spoken argument.

Emotional phrases and word placement are important to consider when evaluating language. Beginning a speech with words that show anger could be off-putting to the listeners. On the other hand, it can set up a situation where the viewers feel a kinship.

There are specific questions you should ask yourself while analyzing a text written in the emotive language style. The following are examples:

- How does the tone or charged language shift as the argument develops?

- Does the emotional language serve to emphasize or downplay the topic being developed?
- How do we know which meanings resonate with our target demographics?

Keep in mind that emotionally charged language and its implications for a particular audience are heavily influenced by factors such as gender, spiritual beliefs, socioeconomic status, and age. Some words can be processed positively by one person but differently by another because they come from vastly different cultural settings.

How do we use emotive language?

Avoid using overly dramatic or inappropriate language. If you pick the right words, the entire statement will retain its meaning. Therefore, there are rules to observe when using emotive phrases and words in any form of communication.

- The error of using too much passionate language is a common pitfall that might turn off your audience.

- Don't be vague as vague language fails to create a reaction from the audience. They start to wonder if you know what you want to convey.

- Keep your language as straightforward as possible; this will let the audience know how you truly feel. Using words that are hard to understand will lead to material that is more difficult to understand overall.

- Words with strong emotional connotations might move your audience to take action. Take advantage of emotive language's persuasive potential to encourage your listeners to do an activity they otherwise would not accept. Anger, for instance, might set off a chain reaction of irritation that compels onlookers to take immediate action.

- Think about the fact that when discussing an individual's work, you must talk about something they are genuinely interested in. Phrases like "hope" and "admiration" might show how much you value their efforts and dedication.

Key takeaways

- People's emotions undergo a wide range of changes when they hear emotionally charged words. A hurtful remark, for instance, might cause actual harm to a good person. Genuinely heartwarming information can also be conveyed, increasing the reader's or listener's joy. To do so, however, you must employ appropriate phrases or words for the particular context.
- Developing your emotional jargon is the most efficient means of boosting your skill in employing emotional verbal language and improving your written emotional language skills as well. Strive to learn more by reading widely and expanding your vocabulary. A wide range of figurative language is available in internet articles and blogs.
- Using the right emotional language can help your audience connect with your work on a deeper level. If you want your words to have more of an impact, work on building your emotional vocabulary.

8

MAKING DIALOGUE PERSONAL

No one can survive on their own, as the old adage says. In fact, having friends and family outside of work and getting along with coworkers is equally important. Building professional connections is crucial. Furthermore, it is beneficial to your social health to make acquaintances at work. However, for some of us, this is easier said than done. Conversing with a stranger for the first time might be nerve-wracking. Don't even bother trying to be their friend. Making first contact with just a "Hello" is pretty straightforward. You'll need the ability to maintain a conversation, though.

Here is how to handle yourself in conversation like a pro to make those crucial connections.

How do you have a stimulating discussion?

Many components make for a great conversation. Some things that can be done to prevent uncomfortable silences are discussed below.

1. Hearing what is being said:

Paying close attention while another person is talking is the goal of active listening. It is common for people to listen with the intent of responding rather than truly hearing what the other person is saying. Using this ability shows the other person that you are aware of what they are saying. It's a mark of maturity and emotional understanding. More of the dialogue will stick in your mind afterward, too. To become a more engaged listener, try paraphrasing what the speaker has just said. More so by keeping my mouth shut and focusing on what others say.

2. Questioning and clarifying:

Using questions to demonstrate your listening skills is a great option. When a conversation is at a standstill, asking pertinent questions to build on the other person's comments will break the ice. Alternatively, you can inquire further about anything you still need to understand or are fully curious about. Again, this demonstrates to the other person that you value their opinion and thoughts.

3. Sharing common ground and interests:

Listen carefully during conversations for evidence of shared experiences. Finding common ground in your interests is a great way to break the ice and keep the discussion going. Suppose you find some areas of commonality in your conversation. In this case, you'll have a much easier time connecting with the other person. This is fundamental to maintaining a natural flow in any conversation.

4. Guiding the conversation toward a specific goal:

It is important to have something specific in mind when talking to someone, whether a coworker you ran into at the supermarket or a stranger at a networking event. Having a purpose in mind guarantees that the conversation will go somewhere and avoid any awkward silences. If the conversation seems to be lagging, you can inject some new material by referring to your intended outcome.

Need help with how to start a conversation?

You can benefit from the advice below to become a more engaging and effective communicator in both business and social situations.

1. Pose a wide variety of inquiries:

Suppose you want to show that you care and are paying attention. Be sure to give the other individual a chance to respond and take charge. They shouldn't feel like they're being questioned.

2. You should stay away from contentious issues:

It's important to be conscious of context and audience at all times. It's best to steer clear of anything that could be misunderstood as offensive or divisive. Discussion topics can range from current events to religious discussions to items on the most recent PTA agenda.

3. Smile:

Beginning a conversation with a smile on your face is incredibly effective. It's always polite to exchange a kind smile with someone you might start a discussion with; doing so will demonstrate your friendliness and openness.

4. Strive for direct eye contact:

Direct eye contact with the other person is a nonverbal cue of interest and participation in the discourse.

Suppose you are constantly preoccupied or appear uninterested in what the other person is saying. In that case, they will assume the same of you.

5. Compliment the recipient:

Complimenting someone is a thoughtful gesture that is always appreciated. Making a person feel good about themselves is as easy as complimenting them. Your discourse will also benefit from this.

Listen carefully to their comments so you can locate real complement possibilities.

6. Seek suggestions or recommendations:

You can always ask for suggestions or guidance if you still need to decide what to talk about. This demonstrates that you are paying attention and respecting their opinion.

7. Don't make too much of an effort:

Listen carefully to your conversation partner and give them plenty of time to talk. If you talk too much, your discussion partner may feel that you only care about yourself.

8. Keep a cheery disposition:

We demonstrate self-control when we keep our spirits up during a conversation. The converse is also true: people are more interested in talking to an upbeat and optimistic individual than a mopey and whiny one.

9. Employ the FORD method:

The abbreviation FORD describes an approach that offers conversation starters. The acronym represents four important aspects of life: family, occupation, recreation, and dreams. If you can recall this acronym, it will serve as a prompt for at least four common-ground conversation starters.

10. Plan ahead for some discussions:

Using well-researched talking points is a surefire way to make any conversation go well. Conversations with coworkers, bosses, and long-time friends can benefit from advanced planning. If you think about what you want to talk about ahead of time, you won't find yourself at a loss for words.

Turning to another direction, precisely what are your thoughts about chat rooms and other online forums?

Standards for effective digital communication would be helpful in today's internet environment. Many misunderstandings arise from sloppy verbal and written exchanges, which lead to misunderstanding the intended meaning.

Avoid misunderstandings by taking these measures

1. Take advantage of available technology:

Use the tools available to you. Make your emails more engaging by altering the background color or by including emojis and GIFs. Incorporating them into your online conversations is a great way to spice things up and stand out from the crowd utilizing the same dull defaults.

2. Make sure you will be able to continue:

Paying close attention to online conversations is just as important as in-person conversations. Pay attention to your verbal exchanges. Don't multitask by talking on the phone and typing simultaneously; the receiver will notice your distraction. It's more than that. You're less likely to communicate clearly when a lot is happening around you.

You can improve the quality of your communications by removing any potential sources of distraction. That way, you will only spend time explaining things to people later.

3. Don't be a time waster:

Make sure you're communicating for a good purpose. If a brief phone call may answer your query or fix your problem, do it that way. It may take some practice before you can determine when to phone and when to send an email; but the benefits to your team's productivity and satisfaction will be worth the effort.

4. Take notes:

taking notes during essential real-time online conversations protects against forgetting important information after the fact. It also saves time by preventing you from having to contact meeting participants again to obtain previously discussed material.

5. Participate in a shared digital experience:

Many of us now have the luxury of working from home. Yet, this freedom may also bring feelings of loneliness and separation. Taking part in online activities can ease this problem. Taking a virtual tour with your friends or coworkers or playing an online game together are also great ways to strengthen your bonds.

6. Do not be shy when making small talk:

It's crucial to remember that small talk is just as vital in online conversations as in personal ones. When communicating online, it's no sweat to get caught up in the business at hand, yet doing so can make conversations appear cold and impersonal.

7. Recognize when to cut a conversation short:

As part of mastering the art of communication, knowing when and how to stop a discussion is also crucial: this includes both in-person and digital interactions. However, putting a stop to discourse in cyberspace is sometimes more complicated. Do your best to interpret the other person's body language during a video call. Think about how you can read the non-verbal signs that indicate it's time to conclude the conversation. It can be yawning, or you might find yourself repeating your words.

Be prepared for appropriate moments by practicing some polite conversation closers

Explain the practical applications of conversational skills in the business world. Pleasant conversations with coworkers has benefits beyond the realm of friendship formation in the workplace. Consider why it is so important in business to be a skilled communicator.

1. Talking increases our ability to influence our own lives and the world around us.

Conversational skills will help you gain influence in the job in various ways. In particular, it aids in the acquisition of referent power by encouraging the development of positive relationships with one's coworkers.

The ability to engage others in meaningful discourse will also increase your clout. Successful communication is a key component of inclusive and effective leadership. Possessing strong verbal communication skills will aid in relaying team objectives and plans. People you're talking to will trust you even more if you do this.

Your credibility as a leader will increase if you can handle challenging conversations well.

2. Building professional relationships is a great way to advance in your field.

Your ability to network will increase if you are good at conversing. Consequently, this will expand your network and help you advance in your profession.

Although our credentials are what get us interviews, it is our interpersonal skills that help us advance in our chosen fields.

3. Good interactions at work increase worker happiness.

Having a conversation is crucial for making and keeping friends at work. Consequently, high morale and group cohesion are the results of cultivating meaningful connections among colleagues.

4. Quality conversations raise productivity and effectiveness:

Pleasant interactions between coworkers improve morale and productivity in the workplace. In addition to boosting productivity, these can also save time. You'll improve your skillset to the point where you can help teach and advance your coworkers. On-the-job training will go more smoothly and take less time if the trainee communicates effectively with their instructors. As a result, we should see increased productivity and efficiency.

But what about the introverted and the shy?

Although being introverted can make it more difficult to initiate a conversation, it is not impossible. We've laid out some approaches that should help.

Get some conversational icebreakers ready

Get some conversation starters ready and try them out. Start conversations with less anxiety and more confidence by planning.

Ask both yes/no and open-ended questions

When you ask a closed question, your conversation partner is restricted in the kinds of answers they can provide. You can only get a yes or no response from someone, for instance, if you ask them a yes or no inquiry. When you ask someone an open-ended question, you aren't placing any restrictions on the possible answers they could supply. Conversations can be extended with the help of some well-placed open-ended questions. It is vital to employ closed and open questions to keep the dialogue moving without hiccups.

Learn to interpret nonverbal cues

In-person interactions rely heavily on body language to express meaning beyond what can be said with words alone. Paying close attention to your discussion partner's body language will help you pick up on subtle but significant social cues. You can utilize body language to keep the atmosphere calm when you know you have to have a challenging conversation.

Use your curiosity

Curiosity can lead to additional question asking, which helps maintain conversational momentum. Conversation starters and subjects can be mined from your insatiable intellectual curiosity. If you choose a topic that intrigues you, you will find it easy to initiate a conversation.

Be kind to yourself

Keep self-compassion and kindness at the lead of your mind at all times. It's important to forgive and retry if you make a fool of yourself in a conversation. It takes bravery to learn how to start a difficult conversation. You will improve with practice even if you fail at anything the first time. Learn how to interact with others and you'll make solid connections.

Understanding how to hold a conversation is crucial in today's digital age. Workplace realities have changed, yet maintaining human connections remains essential. Strengthening your ability to converse will do more than help you connect with your contemporaries. You'll have more clout and feel more assured.

Key takeaways

- Disagreements frequently occur because careless verbal and written communication fails to convey the intended meaning.
- The purpose of active listening is to pay close attention while another person is speaking. The tendency to listen only with an eye on retorting rather than actively taking in what the other person is saying is widespread. Utilizing this skill demonstrates to the other person that you are interested in what they say.
- Mastering the art of conversation is a vital life skill. And just like any other skill, it takes time and effort. The good news is that purposeful practice can help you improve. Never stop working to improve daily. Whether you're looking to improve your conversational abilities, confront your inner critic, or map out your professional future, getting started with personalized guidance today will help you gain further quicker.

9

TYPES OF COMMUNICATION STYLES

Insights into a person's personality can be gleaned from their choice of attire. Despite appearances, we often form opinions about people from what they are donning at the moment. Someone in a neatly pressed suit would be assumed to have an important business appointment, whereas someone in a bathing suit and sandals would be directed to the nearest beach.

The same is true of our modes of communication. Several inferences may be made about a person based on their communication style, including the speaker's mood, disposition, and topic.

While everyone has their distinct sense of style, there are a few broad categories that most people fall into such grunge, chic, hipster, and professional. The same holds for the way we express ourselves verbally.

What are the types of communication styles?

- Passive
- Aggressive
- Passive-aggressive
- Assertive

Even though people tend to choose one of these modes of expression in everyday conversation, they are not bound to it. The speaker's tone and word choice can shift from time to time, leaving listeners gaping and looking puzzled, depending on their state of mind or the impression they're going for.

Passive Communication

Those who want to appear uninterested in a topic will often utilize a passive communication style. They don't voice their thoughts or make it appear as though they agree with everything said.

When asked for their opinion, passive speakers give off uneasy nonverbal communication indicators such as avoiding eye contact, slouching, and shrugging.

Why would someone choose to communicate passively?

Keeping the peace, especially while dealing with conflict, is a significant motivator for passive communication. Although well-intentioned, such a stance often backfires and causes issues for the person doing the passive communication. When someone doesn't express themselves clearly, the other person's words and behaviors can cause them to feel nervous, unhappy, or resentful.

What is it about this method of interaction that makes it so inefficient?

Although words may be spoken in passive communication, the actual thoughts and ideas of the communicator are not expressed, resulting in a lack of information transfer.

If the other person in a conversation with you never expresses their feelings, try to break through their passiveness. If you tend to be a passive communicator, it's time to get your act together. Take into consideration that what you think is important.

Aggressive Communication

In contrast, aggressive communication is at the other end of the spectrum. People with aggressive communication styles are not shy about sharing their thoughts and feelings and often use a commanding tone and volume. People often make direct eye contact, point fingers, and maintain a firm stance when speaking angrily.

Sharing one's thoughts and feelings is the key to effective communication, but aggression in this context is counterproductive. As part of this mode, you may communicate your thoughts or feelings in a hostile and disrespectful manner, infringing on the rights of others.

Why would someone choose to communicate in such a hostile manner?

When people desire to be in command, they typically adopt an aggressive tone of voice. They don't bother to hear what others say, instead issuing orders and demanding compliance. The aggressive communicator may succeed in making the target feel small and irrelevant even if they do respond.

What about this method of interaction that makes it so inefficient?

To communicate effectively with someone, avoid using an angry tone. Aggression is aimed at scaring others away, which is counterproductive in discourse when people are supposed to share and listen to one another's thoughts.

Defend yourself if a hostile speaker addresses you with aggressive language. Forcing someone to listen is challenging but will result in a more fruitful conversation. If you tend to come across as forceful in conversation, make a concerted effort to demonstrate empathy and hear out the perspectives of those around you.

Passive-aggressive Communication

Passive-aggressive communication combines aggressive and passive approaches to language to provide yet another ineffectual kind of interpersonal interaction. Passive-aggressive language is employed when a speaker wants to convey anger but doesn't immediately express it (aggressive).

People who communicate in a passive-aggressive manner may murmur things to themselves in public as though they didn't mean for anybody else to hear them.

Many people who utilize passive-aggressive communication styles also avoid directly addressing the issues that worry them with others. As an example, some people may ignore others or discuss the problem with a third party who isn't involved in the conflict.

For what purposes might one resort to passive-aggressive language?

It's common for people to engage in passive aggression when they have strong feelings about an issue but are concerned about how others will react to them. They would rather not publicly disagree with someone, so they do so with insinuation.

What about this method of interaction that makes it so inefficient?

Passive-aggressive language is inefficient and avoids confrontation. A lack of transparency in expressing thoughts wastes time and undermines the importance of clear communication.

Determine what the aggressive part of the comment means if individuals are passive-aggressive or prod them into telling you how they feel. Refrain from being evasive while expressing your views, especially if they conflict with another person's if you want to avoid being passive-aggressive.

Assertiveness

Many people believe that the most productive method of communication is the assertive one. Strong communicators are respectful of others while still expressing their views, and they speak in a quiet, non-threatening voice and show no signs of hostility. You might be wondering why it's crucial to speak authoritatively.

Assertive communication is encouraged as it emphasizes openness and mutual comprehension. People who communicate assertively take responsibility for their thoughts and actively consider those of others.

Using "I" statements indicates an individual who can confidently express themselves in conversation. They will shift the responsibility away from the person they disagree with and onto themselves.

Why is this method of expression the most productive?

The success of assertive dialogues requires participation from both parties, which is why being direct and confident in your words always pays off. Polite communication improves the quality of the discourse and the flow of information by allowing each participant to voice their thoughts while simultaneously soliciting and considering those of others.

Being forceful is the most productive method of expression, as it avoids unnecessary ambiguity and can be understood without alarm or disrespect. The conversation improves when multiple perspectives are brought to bear, and you can achieve your goals through confident information exchanges.

Communicating assertively implies putting across your ideas without watering them down. Although it is the ideal look, not everyone can pull it off. To become a more confident speaker, consider the following:

Keeping things straight should be your priority

Honesty is the cornerstone of assertive communication skills. When you don't agree with someone, it's tempting to avoid confrontation by avoiding the issue altogether. However, being polite while disagreeing is preferable to agreeing with something you don't believe to be true.

Try to improve your listening skills

When trying to be aggressive, it's important to put yourself in the other people's shoes and see things from their perspective. Listening is the only method for achieving this goal. Always listen attentively and suppress the urge to interrupt a speaker.

To each his own

It's acceptable to agree to disagree if you've done your best to comprehend the other person's viewpoint but still can't accept it as long as proper decorum is maintained.

Make sure you don't freak out

The words of others have the potential to inflame, anger, or distress you. You are a feeling human, and that is not a terrible thing at all. However, if you want to be an effective forceful communicator, you can't let your anger show. Relax your face and voice, and take a few deep breaths.

Get serious about it

Successful, assertive communication requires dedication, like dieting or training a puppy. You can improve your ability to communicate assertively by regularly practicing the strategies mentioned earlier. It will take a lot of trials, and you'll have to exercise patience and determination, but the result is worth it as you'll be a far more persuasive communicator.

Act confidently

There is the constant deployment of a wide variety of comm modes. People's inability to adequately convey their emotions is sometimes the result of feelings of shyness, fear, or both. Try to be confident and aggressive in your interactions. If you want to portray the appropriate image of yourself, this is the way to do it.

Key takeaways

- Passive, aggressive, passive-aggressive, and assertive are all communication styles.
- Assertive communication is seen by many as the most effective interaction style. Effective communicators can voice their opinions while also showing consideration for those who disagree. They don't make hostile gestures or use loud, menacing voices.
- Honesty, improvement, and confidence are key to assertive communication.

10

TONE OF VOICE

Using a sarcastic, insulting, or contemptuous tone can turn otherwise harmless words into ones that hurt and offend the listener. Soft speech can be misunderstood as insecurity, whereas loud speech can be taken as hostility.

You want people to focus on your words rather than how you act. Controlling your tone is essential if you want to accomplish your goals.

The tone of your voice bears more than simply the words you choose to express yourself. The tone of voice is one of the most important nonverbal clues, along with body language and eye contact, that conveys more meaning than the words themselves. Using it effectively can pave the way to more fulfilling personal, professional, and social interactions.

Voice tone might be official or casual, amusing or serious, factual or respectful, assertive or hesitant, or even conversational. However, four components make up your tone of voice in a conversation, and the ability to control your tone and apply it effectively depends upon your aware-ness of these factors.

Pitch

The range of your voice's pitch determines how high or low you can sing or speak. Immaturity and defensiveness may be inferred from a voice that is too high in pitch. In addition, ending a sentence with a higher pitch might make it sound like an inquiry rather than an affirmative statement, which can confuse the other person.

The pitch of your voice is an important aspect of the tone of voice since it allows you to be heard above other people's conversations. A low pitch can make you look more authoritative and serious, even if your words aren't profound. This is useful when trying to make a professional impression or hammer in a point. As a result, how you say things can have the opposite effect. Others may misinterpret your shrill tone as indicating that you don't know what you're trying to say. If others don't trust you, they won't grant the benefit of the doubt when it's about achieving your goals.

Pace

If you and your better half are having a dispute, do you speak more swiftly or slowly than usual? At work or during a formal presentation? It's not enough to dial in your vocal tone; you must watch how quickly you speak. If you talk more slowly, your listeners will easily follow along and absorb your message. The converse is also true; speaking too slowly might be taken incorrectly and offensive. To ensure that your message is understood, you must talk clearly and at a consistent rate.

When addressing a group of people, it's often best to speak at a rate of around half your typical speech rate. It's an excellent way to ensure everyone understands your tone of voice.

The value of a constant and even tempo lies in its ability to enhance concentration. Slow speaking makes it easier for your conversation partner or audience to catch every word. Suppose you need to be wary about your tone and speak quickly while stringing words together. In that case, it will be difficult for your audience to understand what you're saying and remain interested.

Volume

Yelling at your spouse will result in an argument or have the opposite effect and cause them to withdraw from the conversation. This is especially true in personal connections, but it is equally valid in professional and personal talks with friends, family, and strangers. Talking too loudly gives off an aggressive and inconsiderate vibe. You might stress a point by speaking more slowly as an alternative to boosting your volume if you want to emphasize a particular point or give your listeners a moment to process what you just said pause.

Timbre

Timbre is the emotional weight you put behind what you say and the tone of your voice. This will aid the listeners in constructing a foundational comprehension of what you are saying. Spend some time getting to know your voice and practicing vocal control (e.g., frustrated, rushed, happy, sad). You will learn to recognize the underlying attitudes that shape the tone of your voice.

A unique voice can be developed through the use of emotionally charged language. One of the most efficient ways to establish authority when speaking is to shift your perspective from the heart and let your message come through in your words. One of the most efficient ways to establish authority when speaking is to shift your view from the heart and let your message come through in your words.

Why is tone of voice so important?

Tone of voice incorporates everything you say. It's how you come across to others and the impression you leave with your words. Consider how your vocal "fingerprint" may reveal so much about you and your character. How certain are you? Optimistic? Intriguing? Respectful? Compassionate? Your conversation tone conveys all of this and more.

To a large extent, others can infer your personality from the tone of your voice. Like you, they are human beings who respond best to upbeat, optimistic language. However, the impact of your tone of voice increases dramatically in romantic interactions.

How do you develop a friendly tone of voice?

Changing Your Speaking Patterns

When you breathe from your diaphragm, you can better modulate your tone. A more friendly tone of voice can be achieved by knowing when to speak more slowly and quickly or by raising or lowering your voice. If you want more control, try breathing deeply and powerfully from your abdomen. Face the mirror and look at yourself while you breathe to see if you're using your diaphragm (the muscle below your lungs). You aren't using your diaphragm properly if your shoulders and chest rise as you breathe in and out. If you place your palm on your stomach and press it outward while you breathe in, you'll be training your diaphragm to do the work.

Make sure to use a range of pitches in your vocals.

Don't just drone on and on. Alternate between high and low pitches while you speak. By raising the pitch of your voice on keywords, you can reassure your audience while a lower voice tone adds a soothing effect to your words. Make a high note to end a question and a low note to end a statement. Statements that are closed with an exaggerated tone give the impression that the speaker does not fully believe them.

Maintaining a cordial demeanor calls for a conversational voice that varies in pitch. Speaking in a very high pitch could make people wonder if you swallowed a helium balloon. However, speak at a very low volume. Your listener can feel that you are interested in something other than what they say.

Keep your audience interested by speaking slowly.

If you talk too rapidly, people may feel that you want to wrap up the conversation as soon as possible. Instead, it would help if you spoke slowly so your audience could catch every word. This will show that you greatly value your time with them and your conversation. You can get your point across without spending thirty seconds on each word, instinctively slowing down when you become more self-aware of your velocity. If you want your listener to stay up with you, use a few pauses.

Don't come off as hostile by speaking more softly.

Feeling like you're being yelled at is one of life's worst experiences. Avoid shouting and speak at a level others can easily hear you. You can alleviate this by practicing diaphragmatic breathing or measured exhalations that allow you to be heard without straining. There's something wrong if you have to yell to be heard.

Speaking clearly will help your audience understand what you're saying.

If you don't stress each syllable when you say it, your audience cannot catch what you're saying. Worse yet, they might conclude that you're deliberately trying to convey a message they can't pick up on, and this may cause them to become bewildered and irritated. Try saying tongue twisters to yourself for five minutes every morning and night to work on your pronunciation.

It's a good idea to record yourself working on your alterations. You can record yourself talking using your phone or a camera. Think about the volume, pace, and tone of your voice. Change and adapt with each new recording.

Having a Friendly Conversation

Just by smiling, you can instantly become more approachable. The muscles in your face relax, and your skin expands when you smile. If you do this, your tone will improve immediately. When you smile, you instantly put the other person at ease. The next time you're in the restroom, try uttering a few lines while flashing a wide grin over your face.

To appear approachable:

- Keep your body relaxed and your posture straight.
- Stop hunching your shoulders and straightening your back and arms.
- Maintain an upright posture while talking.
- Create an upbeat and friendly vibe with your body language instead.
- If you find your arms dangling at your sides while conversing, you can prevent this by lacing your fingers together in front of your body. Still, this posture is more welcoming than crossing one's arms across one's chest.

Take the time to listen to someone to demonstrate empathy. Be genuinely curious about what the other person is saying as you converse with them. As they speak, nod your head and focus on their face. By demonstrating your concern, you can keep the discussion light and pleasant even when you aren't the one leading it. Maintain interest by asking pertinent questions based on what they've already said.

Key takeaways

- Maintain an even flow of discussion by talking to each other. Don't let the talk become one-sided; keep the exchange going. It would help if you didn't bore people to death with an hour-long tale. Instead, spend time together to learn more about one another and catch up on how you're both doing.

- Compliment people sincerely if you want to be kind. Use a pleasant tone and word choice when you communicate. Give the other individual the benefit of a positive impression. It will come across as false if you lie to someone just to be kind. Don't engage in idle chitchat or constant griping. These behaviors will transform even the most pleasant chat into a complaining fest in no time.

- You should watch your tone when complimenting someone to avoid being too pushy. Excessive use of the wrong words will cause you to speak in a sarcastic tone. If you say, "I love those earrings!" with an extremely high-pitched "love," your listener might see it as a joke about their earrings.

11

PRACTICE PRONUNCIATION

Numerous elements influence effective communication. The most basic requirement is proper language pronunciation, and English pronunciation is covered in this chapter. There are many words in the language to pronounce properly. Even if we operate in a workplace where English is spoken, we could ignore pronunciation and assume we got it right until they complain that we didn't.

Making mistakes is okay, but doing so repeatedly is not, and it needs fixing. People might have an unfavorable initial impression of you if they can't understand you due to faulty pronunciation, especially at work. Who likes listening to someone who only a select few can understand?

Speaking and hearing, talking and listening, encoding and conveying your message, and receiving and decoding other people's messages, are all interactive aspects of communication. When you mispronounce English words, others around you feel uncomfortable because they can't comprehend the majority of what you say. I'll be going into more detail about this in this chapter.

It may significantly affect how you feel psychologically. You might experience awkwardness and shame and even question your ability to speak English well. Fear and self-doubt are the seeds of all motivational evil. Once you lose interest in working on your English communication abilities, that's it. You fall into a rabbit hole of self-criticism, uncertainty, and timidity. And to get out of it and renounce requires a lot of bravery (or the expertise of a native English coach).

You now understand why it's crucial to study and practice the pronunciation of English words. Right or wrong, there is no such thing as perfect pronunciation. Even natural English speakers blunder or have accents that cause them to sound foreign. It's okay, too.

Instead of sounding like a native English speaker, your objective should be to speak as closely as you can to a standard pronunciation so that listeners of all languages—native and non-native—can comprehend what you are saying. Choose it based on your personal preferences and career objectives, then go for it.

Pronunciation vs. Accent

I should now provide a few clarifications in this context. Making the sounds of the letters and articulating words with your tongue, lips, and throat is known as pronunciation. It also involves raising or lowering your voice as you speak and emphasizing the appropriate words and sentences (this is intonation). Does the distinction between pronunciation and accent exist? The answer is both yes and no. Yes, because pronunciation is part of an accent, and "no" because if you have a foreign accent, you might use different words for the same thing or use different grammar and syntax.

Additionally, your accent and pronunciation can be affected if you don't speak English as your first language. It might have various sounds that change how you pronounce English-language sounds. In any event, remember that good pronunciation requires physical, not mental, skills, and it depends upon how you use your throat, tongue, and lips muscles. So, be easy on yourself and focus on your pronunciation; you must educate yourself on how to do it correctly.

I'll provide some exercises, tools, and ideas to help you pronounce words more clearly. Still, they all come under one of these three categories:

- Discovering the proper pronunciation
- Honing your pronunciation via practice and
- Observation of your speech patterns and errors.

You must first become familiar with word pronunciation. You all know how to pronounce words in English, although this is frequently only the result of repeated hearing. You learn how to pronounce the words over time and as you engage in more discussions in English. This approach is dangerous since you can never be sure if you understand when you hear a native English speaker speak.

I advise being familiar with the International Phonetic Alphabet (IPA). Instead of spelling out the words, this tool assists you in comprehending how to pronounce them. You can accurately guess the sounds 100% of the time because it uses various symbols and letters to differentiate them. If you use a dictionary, it very certainly includes the IPA pronunciation for each word.

Now that you know how to complete your homework with the IPA's assistance, you are prepared to begin evaluating your performance. It would help if you had both practical examples and the theory, such as listening to how English-speaking native speakers pronounce words.

Watch a TV program or TED lecture on YouTube, for instance, when the speaker is a natural English speaker.

When they utter specific sounds in words, pay attention to the movements of their mouth and lips. Perhaps they have pouted lips or round lips. Even though you can't see how they use their tongue or throat, observing how their lips are formed will help you pronounce words correctly. Then, while facing a mirror, practice your words and sounds. Combine the IPA sounds with the native speaker techniques you observed. Attempt to mimic them. If you like, use your smartphone to record a video of yourself (video is way better than audio). Then, play it back to check if you did it right (and your words came out correctly) or made a mistake. Repeat after me. The first step in getting better is recognizing your faults. Remember to give yourself a warm pat on the back for pronouncing the words correctly. Always be motivated by yourself.

The enjoyable part now is practicing and honing your pronunciation.

Word sound breakdown is a wonderful place to start. Break the word down into syllables and the syllables into sounds rather than pronouncing the entire word all at once, which can sometimes result in mumbling if the word is long. Practice each sound and syllable one at a time, then repeat the process. When it comes to life in general, breaking up big goals or undertakings into smaller, more manageable, and doable steps is a strategy that can help you succeed. Try saying the word out loud one more time.

Pay attention to any words or sounds you have problems pronouncing.

For added assistance, write the words in syllables, with a line separating each syllable in a word. Additional advice: put your finger beneath your chin and speak the word if you're unsure of the syllable count. A new syllable is added every time your chin brushes against your finger. Try using the word "syllable" alone. "Syl-la-ble." Your finger was touched three times by your chin. Isn't it a lot simpler now?

Okay, this is difficult yet useful. If you have practiced saying a word that you find challenging, try to visualize it. Close your eyes and imagine where your tongue and lips should be placed to produce the sound. You need to make your lips round and project them somewhat forward if you've observed how native English speakers pronounce the challenging phoneme "sh," as in the word "English." Then make the motions while uttering the word. Always keep in mind that perfecting a skill requires repeated practice. I advise performing this exercise frequently while closing your eyes. It's crucial to pay attention to the motions and activities occurring inside your mouth, and it might be more challenging to do it. At the same time, your eyes are open since you are more susceptible to distraction from outside visual stimuli.

Exaggeration, while unmindful, can be used to your advantage in pronunciation.

I'll give you an example from real life. Actors frequently exaggerate in the theater. The director often yells to the actors during the rehearsals, "exaggerate!" because the theatre is a type of art where oral words and facial gestures add to the performers' competence. In short, increase or dial up the tone. If the performers are meant to laugh, they must laugh extremely loudly. In the original Greek definition of the genre, this is exactly what drama is all about. The same is true of how you pronounce words. Of course, you don't have to be theatrical, but you can emphasize the sounds that make your life difficult.

To put it another way, there are two options: increase the volume of the sounds until you get uncomfortable. The second option is to become more timid by pronouncing words and sounds confidently and softly. Which option would you pick? Select option #1. There is no justification for feeling silly. Contrarily, making loud, assertive noises with intricate sounds earns you bonus points. Furthermore, the locals won't even notice because they will consider it natural.

Even though the phrase is still somewhat fresh, this activity is excellent. What exactly is shadowing, and how does it help with pronunciation? Using this method, you listen to someone speak in English (or any other language) and immediately repeat what they say. To their speech, it is like a shadow or echo. You could laugh at it or question if it works. Yes, especially when it comes to pronunciation. You can use it to practice in an environment similar to real life. Still, I wouldn't advise using it to learn a new language or enhance your English. Since it's all about muscles, as I've already explained, the faster you train them, the quicker you progress.

Another fascinating aspect of shadowing is that it can help you improve your overall English-speaking abilities, including pronunciation, stress, and intonation. The latter are crucial components of speaking English naturally and confidently, so giving them a shot is worthwhile. The process is straightforward:

- Pick your preferred Netflix show, movie, YouTube clip, or podcast.
- Activate the English subs or keep the transcript close at hand.
- Try to keep up by repeating as they speak.
- Although it might not be simple at first, as you advance, you'll find it simpler to keep up with speed.

While waiting for the doctor or the metro, I have found myself in several seemingly unpleasant circumstances, where I have read aloud a text written in a different language. That was how I would exercise my muscles. If you did it, it would be beneficial for sure. You can increase the scope of your reading practice once you have mastered the first six suggestions I'm sharing, you will feel more assured. Read the texts aloud on your preferred English news website or online publication.

Most importantly, while learning new terminology, you will improve your pronunciation privately, free from criticism. Try not to be too self-critical on yourself. Keep practicing until you master each sound, even if you still make mistakes or have trouble with some of them. Recognize each sound you have mastered and continue the conscious practice. Plan to read English literature aloud for 15 minutes daily as a routine. Be bold and look up a word in a dictionary to learn how to pronounce it with the aid of the IPA letters if you need help. If you're still unsure, ask a native English speaker to keep an eye on you and fix your errors. An English professional coach can be helpful if you are still looking for one.

Most English language learners think speaking more quickly makes them sound more proficient. I've got news for you: this is untrue. Aligning the body and mind is a necessary component of effective English communication. Speaking too quickly will cause your brain to strain and make you sound worse than you might imagine. It's sometimes simple to communicate in a language different than your mother tongue, but speaking quickly can easily overwhelm you. Your body will feel less comfortable with an anxious mind.

As a result, your muscles will be strained and rigid, including the ones you use to speak. Have you ever seen performers, singers, or presenters use their mouths to perform particular exercises that more closely resemble humorous facial expressions? They do it to unwind their body's muscles and facilitate a soft, smooth voice. That also applies to you. When you can talk more slowly in the first place, you do not need to force yourself into this situation. Speaking more slowly aids with breathing, and the brief pauses will allow you to refocus on your English pronunciation and message quickly.

The enjoyable part is about to start! I decided to wrap this advice list with two entertaining techniques to improve pronunciation. You should have a flexible, formal learning environment; but above all, you must include opportunities to enjoy yourself and the work. Practicing with well-known tongue twisters is one of them; they can be of great assistance to you. You may need help pronouncing most of them because they have similar sounds crammed together. Additionally, some employ so-called "minimal pairs," or pairs of words with the same pronunciation but for one sound (such as tap/top or beat/bit). When you feel more in control, practice the tongue twisters slowly and then pick up the pace.

What about music? Which musician or group is your favorite? Pick up your favorite songs, play them on your computer or phone, and start singing along! You can do it quickly because you are familiar with the songs. If you need help remembering the exact lyrics, you can locate them on Google. Singing may be enjoyable, soothing, and entertaining while it helps you improve your English (even if your voice is terrible like mine). A win-win circumstance!

It works because finding the appropriate words and building sentences is no longer a burden. This allows you to concentrate simply on the words and their pronunciation. Sing louder while paying close attention to how you pronounce the words. It is similar to the way the vocalist performs! It combines shadowing with reading aloud from texts. The pressure or fear you experience when speaking English can be removed by this two-in-one enjoyable activity, allowing you to practice without being self-conscious or insecure because you now merit it and possess the necessary English communication skills!

Key takeaways

- Remember that you must invest time and effort into making these tips and strategies effective because they are not quick fixes. But if you do, they can be effective.
- Remember to sound as near the norm as possible so everyone can understand you and value your opinions.
- Right or wrong, there is no such thing as perfect pronunciation. Even natural English speakers blunder or have accents that cause them to sound foreign.

12

BODY LANGUAGE

Our body language and facial expressions, among other nonverbal indicators, tell others a great deal about us. Body language refers to the nonverbal signs we utilize to convey meaning. A lot of what we say to one another daily is communicated through nonverbal cues, and up to 65% of all communication may be conveyed through body language.

Why is body language significant?

Understanding oneself and others through body language is beneficial since it informs us of potential human emotions in a particular circumstance. Additionally, body language can be used to convey feelings or intentions.

In addition to learning to read body language, it's important to pay attention to indications apparent in the overall context. A better strategy is to keep an eye on the signs rather than fixating on one particular move. To help you understand nonverbal behaviors, this chapter analyzes the functions that body language plays in communication, provides examples of body language, and explains the meaning of each.

Think about how much a simple change in a person's countenance can be conveyed. It's possible to show acceptance and happiness with a smile, and a frown is a facial expression of displeasure or discontent.

There are instances when our outward appearance reveals more about our inner state than we intended. Others may not believe you when you say you're feeling okay, even if that's what you're telling them. People's faces may tell a lot about their feelings: happiness, grief, rage, surprise, disgust, fear, confusion, enthusiasm, desire, or disdain. We can tell whether or not someone is credible based on the expression on their face.

Psychology research has shown several fascinating things regarding body language. A slightly raised brow and a smile are the most trustworthy facial expressions. Experts have conjectured that this expression conveys warmth and confidence.

Another one of the most widely used types of body language consists of facial expressions. Around the world, there are common ways of expressing fear, anger, grief, and happiness.

According to research by Paul Ekman, many facial expressions associated with specific emotions, such as happiness, rage, fear, surprise, and sadness are universal. Research suggests that we infer intellect from a person's expressions and features. According to one study, people with narrower faces and more pronounced noses were more likely to be considered intellectual. People who were happy and smiling were perceived to be smarter than those who were furious.

Because they can tell much about a person's feelings or thoughts, the eyes are usually called the "windows to the soul."

Observing another person's eye movements while conversing with them is a natural and crucial step in communication.

Common cues to look out for include how often someone blinks, whether their pupils are dilated and if they are making direct eye contact or avoiding your gaze. Paying attention is the key to understanding someone's body language. Any of the following eye signals should be watched for.

When someone speaks to you and stares into your eyes, it shows they are engaged and paying attention. However, sustained eye contact can appear dangerous. But if they look away frequently, it could mean they are distracted, uncomfortable, or trying to mask their genuine feelings.

Although blinking is a normal reflex, you should discern if someone blinks excessively or too little. People frequently blink more quickly when anxious or uneasy; infrequently blinking could signify that someone is consciously attempting to control their eye movements. A poker player might, for instance, blink less frequently to appear unimpressed with the hand he was given.

A very delicate nonverbal communication cue can be the size of the pupils. While environmental light levels regulate pupil dilation, emotions occasionally induce minute pupil size adjustments. You may be familiar with the term "bedroom eyes," which refers to the gaze someone makes when they are attracted to another person. For instance, noticeably dilated eyes can signify attention or even arousal.

Mouth gestures and attitudes are also significant for interpreting body language.

For instance, when someone chews on their bottom lip, it might signify anxiety, dread, or insecurity. If someone is coughing or yawning, covering one's mouth may be an attempt to be polite, but it could also be an attempt to hide an unflattering scowl.

Although smiling is one of the best body language signals, it may also be taken in various ways. A grin can be sincere or a way to convey cynicism, sarcasm, or fake delight.

Keep in mind the following lip and mouth cues when interpreting body language:

- **Lips pursed:** tightening of the lips may be a sign of dislike, approval, or mistrust.

- **Lip biting:** when someone is upset, worried, or anxious, they may bite their lips.

- **Covering the mouth:** people may cover their mouths to prevent smiles or smirks when they want to conceal an emotional response.

- **Turned up or down:** minor alterations in the mouth can also serve as oblique cues to how someone is feeling. People may feel cheerful or optimistic if their mouths are slightly tilted. On the other hand, a mouth slightly turned down can signify melancholy, displeasure, or even a grimace.

One of the most straightforward and blatant forms of body language are gestures.

Common and simple ones include waving, pointing, and using the fingers to denote numerical values. For example, giving a thumbs-up or a peace sign may have an entirely different meaning in another country than in the United States since gestures may be culturally specific. A few instances of typical motions and their potential meanings are provided below:

- Clenched fists can signify either fury or camaraderie, depending upon the circumstance.
- The thumbs up and thumbs down signs of approval and displeasure are frequently employed.
- Okay, or "all right" can be expressed by connecting the thumb and index finger in a circle and extending the other three fingers.

However, in various regions of Europe, the identification signal is employed to signify that you are worthless. The sign is a crude gesture in various South American nations.

In some nations, the V sign, made by lifting the index and middle fingers apart to form a V shape denotes victory or peace. When the back of the hand is turned outward, the symbol in the UK and Australia has an insulting connotation.

Additionally, the legs and arms can be used to communicate non-verbally. Arms crossed might be a sign of defensiveness. Crossing one's legs away from another may be a sign of disliking or unease with that person. If one is trying to appear smaller or less dominant, keeping one's arms close to one's body is a possible strategy, whereas opening one's arms wide is a possible strategy for drawing attention to oneself.

Pay attention to some of the following messages that the arms and legs may send while interpreting body language:

- Crossed arms may be an indication of defensiveness, self-preservation, or closed-off-ness.
- Standing with the hands on the waist can either show that a person is prepared and in control, or it could be interpreted as hostility.
- A person clasping their hands behind their back may be experiencing boredom, anxiety, or even anger.
- Fingers tapping quickly or fidgeting suggest boredom, impatience, or frustration.
- Legs crossed can signify that someone feels isolated or needs some privacy.

Body language also include vital cues from the way we hold our bodies.

The term "posture" describes how we keep our bodies and entire physical appearance. A person's posture can reveal a lot about their feelings. Posture serves as a cue about their personality, such as whether the person is assertive, receptive, or subservient. For instance, sitting up straight shows that someone is focused and paying attention to what is happening. Conversely, hunching forward when seated can suggest that a person is bored or uninterested.

Try to pay attention to the indications that a person's posture provides. Maintaining an open posture entails leaving the body's trunk exposed. Postures like this convey friendliness, receptivity, and readiness. Closed posture includes concealing the body's trunk, frequently hunching forward, and maintaining crossed arms and legs. This kind of posture may signal anxiousness, hatred, and unfriendliness.

Have you ever come across the phrase "needing personal space"? Have you ever felt uneasy when someone approaches you too closely? Anthropologist Edward T. Hall first used the term "proxemics" to describe how far apart people are when interacting. The physical space between people can convey as much nonverbal information as body language and facial expressions. Hall outlined four levels of social distance that exist in various contexts.

- 6 to 18 inches is the 'intimate distance.
- This degree of physical separation frequently denotes a more intimate connection or higher level of familiarity between people. It typically happens during close physical contact, including embracing, speaking, or caressing.
- 1.5 to 4 feet, depending upon the individual.
- This kind of physical separation typically occurs between relatives or close friends. The degree of closeness in a relationship can be determined by how closely two individuals can stand to one another while conversing.
- 4 to 12 feet is the social distance.

- This degree of physical separation is frequently employed with acquaintances.

You might feel more at ease interacting up close with someone you know reasonably well, such as a coworker you see frequently.

When you don't know the other person very well, such as someone who only crosses your path once a month, like a mailman, keeping ten to twelve feet between you both may seem more comfortable.

- 12 to 25 feet for public spaces.
- In public speaking contexts, this level of physical separation is frequently used. Such instances include speaking in front of a classroom full of pupils or delivering a presentation at work.

It is also significant to remember that cultures differ in how much personal space is required for people to feel at ease. One frequently mentioned example is the distinction between individuals from Latin and North American cultures. While North Americans need greater personal space while interacting, people from Latin countries typically feel more at ease standing closer together.

In social interactions, body language has many different functions. It can make the following things easier:

- Gaining someone's trust can be accomplished through making eye contact, nodding your head in agreement while being listened to, or even unintentionally copying their body language.

- Your message will be received differently depending on your voice tone, how you interact with the audience through hand and arm motions, body language, and the space you occupy.
- Truth-telling: When a person's actions do not correspond to what they are saying, we may infer that they are hiding information or perhaps not being completely honest about their feelings.

Our body language can communicate a lot about our emotional state. For instance, do you have a reclined position, or are your lips pursed or jaw clenched? This could indicate that something about the surroundings you're in right now is setting you off. Your body may let you know you're stressed, unsafe, or experiencing other feelings.

But remember that you might sometimes be wrong in your interpretation of another person's body language.

What can a person's body language tell you about them?

When someone feels nervous, furious, excited, or any other emotion, their body language may reveal it. It could also imply character qualities (i.e., whether someone is shy or outgoing). However, body language can be deceptive and depends on a person's attitude, energy, and environment.

For example, if someone isn't looking you in the eyes, it doesn't necessarily mean they are untrustworthy. However, this is only sometimes the case. They may be preoccupied and thinking elsewhere. Or, once more, there might be a cultural disparity at work.

But how might nonverbal communication be enhanced?

Being attentive is the first step in enhancing your nonverbal communication. See if you can observe the physical cues of others in addition to your own.

You could tend to glance at the ground when someone tells you a story. Instead, try making eye contact and even cracking a small smile to demonstrate that you are open and engaged in the conversation.

Finding balance is the key to effective body language use. For instance, you are grasping someone's hand relatively forcefully before a job interview can convey professionalism. However, if you grab it too firmly, it could hurt or annoy the other person. Always keep in mind how others may be feeling.

Continue to improve your emotional intelligence along the way. It is frequently simpler to detect how others are receiving you the more in touch you are with your feelings. When someone is open and responsive, or on the other side of the coin, if they are closed-off and need some space, you'll be able to tell.

We use body language when we feel a specific way. For instance, studies have shown that those with better self-esteem who are in happy mood will sit or stand up straight compared to those with slumped postures who are under stress.

Of course, a full image is frequently painted by verbal and nonverbal communication, as well as the environment of the situation.

Appropriate nonverbal cues vary depending upon the situation; there is no one-size fits-all answer. But if you remain attentive and show respect, you'll be well on your path to learning how to read body language.

Key takeaways

- Understanding body language can significantly improve your ability to interact with others and decipher what they are saying. While it may be tempting to analyze nonverbal cues individually, it's crucial to consider how they relate to verbal communication, other nonverbal cues, and the context.
- To use body language effectively, finding a middle ground is essential.
- Additionally, you can hone your nonverbal communication to communicate your feelings to others more effectively without ever having to speak a word.

13

KNOW YOUR AUDIENCE

If you are attempting to communicate your experiences, viewpoints, and conclusions comprehend your words, examples, or frames of reference to others, it is essential to understand who these people are. Try to recall the most recent instance when you and another individual had difficulty understanding one another. In line with the experience of the vast majority of us, most likely it was not long ago.

The issues that arise from human contact are not the fault of individual people. Before we can improve our ability to communicate with one another, we need to gain an understanding of the benefits and drawbacks of language. For a message to be compelling, the person conveying it needs to consider not just their objectives but also the objectives and preferences of those to whom it is being directed.

Before you can successfully persuade someone of anything, it's necessary to be able to speak their language, both literally and symbolically. This doesn't imply you have to abandon your core beliefs or perspectives. Instead, it indicates that you must alter how you communicate with your audience and the information you provide to build a stronger connection. This is more complex than it sounds, particularly when you're trying to communicate with a diverse group within an organization or on a team. Therefore, the issue that arises is: where do you begin?

First determine who you are writing or speaking to for before beginning

When preparing for a presentation or memorandum, establish a list of the various types of people who will be listening. Keep this list open-ended. Consider everyone, including subordinates and superiors, as appropriate. Remember to think about those who will be reading your work.

Consider the various subsets that make up your target market.

- What do they have in common? What sets them apart from one another?

- How much prior knowledge do they already possess on the topic?

- Think about the things that concern them.

While working on finding a solution to a problem, bear in mind their point of view and what is significant to them. Think about the knowledge they could benefit from, how it pertains to the topic, and what intrigues them. Putting yourself in their position will make it easier for you to formulate a message that will appeal to them, conveyed it in a manner that will compel them to pay attention and take action.

Consider the most important pieces of information they require.

No matter how crucial it is to adapt your messages and delivery to your intended audience's specific characteristics, it would be best to keep track of the information you are trying to communicate. Always keep in mind the message you want them to walk away with. Do all you can to provide the information they require in a straightforward and easy-to-understand format.

Next, determine what you want to occur as a direct outcome of the dialogue that you have had.

People need to be told the facts, but they also need to be motivated and interested in what they hear for effective communication. When you are holding your next presentation or writing, keep this in mind. Consider the information you would like others to take away from your presentation. Why would they want have to offer you? That "ask" is being repeated over and over for emphasis. The most effective communication method motivates individuals to take action, and it takes the form of a direct request.

Figure out the most effective strategy to disseminate the information.

Early on, we are instilled with the belief that "everything has its time and place" (whatever the activity may be). This proverb can also be utilized as a tool for having fruitful interactions.

Holding a town hall meeting or gathering your team together is a good idea if you want to inform people about a significant shift in the way things have been done in the past. Think about disseminating information that people need to know frequently but isn't likely to make them anxious by way of a memo, an electronic newsletter, etc. depending upon the means you have available. People have a greater need for an interactive environment or work channel when the message they are receiving is complex.

Consider how you might reach your target market and compel them to take action.

We are finally getting to the meat and potatoes of what it means to have a solid understanding of target demographics. Consider the people you are likely to want to listen to what you have to say. Think of a narrative you might tell them to connect or as a way to demonstrate how their activities affect the firm. Either way, this will help them understand the importance of their roles. At this point, you can leave your audience with a crystal-clear action while also making your thesis more persuasive.

Key takeaways

- To better communicate with one another, we need to know the advantages and disadvantages of language. The efficacy of a message depends upon the sender taking into account not only their own goals but also the goals and preferences of the recipients.
- Thinking like your audience will support how you deliver a message that will resonate with them and communicate it to get their attention and prompt them to take the desired action.
- Knowing your target demographics and adapting your message to that audience's specific interests and requirements is ultimately the most important step in the process. If you approach your message with that frame of mind, connecting with the people listening to you will be much simpler. This is true regardless of the content of your message.

14

ORGANIZING THOUGHTS FOR SPEECH

G etting your thoughts in order may be one of the hardest things you'll ever have to do, both now and in the future. How you organize things in your house or business is very different from how you organize your thoughts. You can only grab a group of ideas like a pen cup full of pencils. You also can't put your thoughts in a box like you would clothes or papers. Either give these ideas a physical form or let your mind organize and process them.

There are many ways to write down all your great little ideas. It's important to stop thinking and get things done. In this chapter, I will give you a list of seventeen different ways to organize your thoughts. Some of these ways to organize your thoughts are simple and more useful than others, while others are more creative. Some techniques let you actively look at your ideas from a different point of view, while others require you to be more detached.

This list of ways to organize will help you whether you're putting together a party, a to-do list, your life, or just trying to figure out what's going on in your work, relationships, finances, health, etc. If you choose the approach or approaches you like best, you will soon be on your way to coordinating your ideas.

You will always go right if you organize your thoughts methodically and step-by-step. Sometimes, just writing down a mental list can make something black and white.

Regarding your ideas, there is not a single bit of doubt in the world: you can see everything that is bothering you right now.

When you need to figure out your thoughts, the following are great ways to do it. After you have an idea or thought, you can easily organize, evaluate, and change it as needed by writing it down on sticky notes, index cards, or a piece of paper.

Put a couple of notes on the wall

For this activity, you will need a clean wall, something to write with, and a few stacks of sticky notes. Put a Post-it note on the wall and write one idea on it. Keep this pattern going; but from now on, only write one idea per note.

After you've cleared your mind, take three big steps away from the wall. What do you see? You need to see something obvious; and after that, you can start putting your sticky notes in piles. This activity is about making sense of your thoughts, so you can put them in any order you want.

Plot out what you think

Drawing a mind map is an easy way to see how ideas fit together. Mind maps are likely something you have seen before, and they center on one main idea and branch out to include other ideas.

You will need a blank paper or notepad. Make a circle around your central concept and write it there. The next step is to draw a line that starts in the middle of the circle and goes all the way out until it touches the paper. Find your central thought and write a thought that goes with it at the end of this line. As you think of new ideas, add them to your map.

As you work on your map, it is helpful to make smaller maps with similar themes to help you organize your thoughts.

Write things down on index cards

Index cards have been used to take notes for a long time. You will need a set of lined or blank index cards and a pen or marker. You can put your ideas in order in one of two ways.

The first is to write one idea on each index cards. This is a lot like the sticky notes method. After writing down your ideas on index cards, you can move them around in any way you want to see your data in a new way.

The other option is to write the main idea on the front of an index card and then put supporting details under the main idea. Again, you can shuffle and rearrange index cards to look at your ideas in a new way.

Make a checklist

Lists are a time-tested method of capturing and organizing thoughts. To make your list sound more impressive, you can get creative. You are merely collecting data for further processing.

The most appropriate action now is to locate some paper, a notepad, and a writing instrument. Create a new line for each concept. Only stop writing once you've run out of things to say. When you're done, take a step back and look at your list. You should expect your list to have some links or things in common.

At this point, you can either make new lists that branch off your original one or draw lines between the items on your original list.

Do a percentage chart

You must know what a pie chart is. These diagrams are in the shape of a pie or circle, with different shades of dark showing various amounts of data (such as money, food, survey responses, or even winning sports teams).

To use this method, you only need a pencil, a piece of paper, or a notepad. Create one large circle in the middle of the paper, then draw smaller circles inside it to represent each concept. Before you commit to a final plan, make sure to double-check your work for coherence. Are some ideas more important, important right now, or timely than others? If you have any ideas, be sure to label them as such in your pie chart.

How to organize your thoughts in unique ways

Are you looking for other ways to organize your thoughts? Why not use your creativity to put all your great ideas, "aha!" moments, and brilliant thoughts in order? Using your creativity can help you see your thoughts and ideas differently.

Organizing your thoughts from a creative point of view can also be a fun process.

The following are some strategies that should help you alter your thought processes. These concepts may appear bizarre or even ridiculous at first, but what do you have to lose by giving them a shot? Use these strategies, and you might be pleasantly amazed by the results.

Handwrite a letter

Writing letters is an art form all by itself. When writing, it's important to consider how you want to present your ideas. This is your official notice that you need to start writing letters again. Step one: do what's written here.

Prepare some white paper and a pen. Put away your mobile device and put your PC to sleep. You'll write a letter to a close friend in the next few minutes. Remember that you're writing this letter to yourself and not to anyone else; it's just a way to get your thoughts on paper.

How would you explain to a friend what's going on in your head right now, with everything that's going on? Find out which ideas are related and which are not. Write the letter taking as much time as you need.

If you can't get your thoughts in order, try writing a letter from your "stream of consciousness." As you consider the situation, jot down whatever ideas occur to you. There is no requirement for alteration or an alternative action on your part. When you feel like quitting, stop writing.

Create a collage

Do you learn best by seeing or hearing? Using different pictures and images, you can make a collage that illustrates your ideas. Because it will take more work, you should give yourself a lot of time.

Start by gathering all the old magazines, newspapers, flyers, cards, and other printed materials you can find around your house. You will also need scissors, a poster board or a thick sheet of paper stock, a glue stick, glue or rubber cement, and a glue bottle.

You might find something interesting in the stacks of books and magazines you have on hand. These can be words, pictures, colors, lines, or shapes. Your wants and needs are important. After cutting out your pieces, take time to arrange them on the poster board. Once you're happy with the layout, put glue on everything and take a look at your work.

Make a list of what's in the book

Do you ever want to fill your head with a thick book? To go all the way with this, why try writing a table of contents? By following this procedure, you are forced to think seriously about how your ideas are organized and clear.

Find a pen or pencil and some paper or a notebook. You could also use a word processor for this task.

Envision yourself in charge of creating the book's table of contents. Whose proposal should go into the spotlight first? Which one comes after the others? When furnishing a space, what should be placed in the middle? When creating a table of contents, you have complete creative freedom.

Put together a timeline

Putting your thoughts on a calendar or timeline will help you look at things in a new light. It's like looking back at your thoughts, ideas, experiences, and efforts. For this task, you will need paper and a pen. A calendar or planner that has seen better days can help you organize your thoughts.

Here's what you do: choose the best timing method for your needs. Creating a calendar, any combination of the years, months, days, and even times of day is possible. When you've settled on a strategy, divide your thoughts among the available slots. Rank your concerns from most pressing to least important.

Put your thoughts and events in any order that makes the most sense, but remember to take lots of notes to keep track of what you're doing!

Record your voice

A simple way to record your inner monologue is to keep a journal or make a voice recording. You can hear what you are thinking and how you think.

For this method, you need an electronic recording device, any one that can record sound, like a voice recorder, audio software, or an app on your phone or tablet. Start by writing down your thoughts and ideas as soon as you feel ready.

Don't worry about listening to the tape right away. Put it away for a few days and then come back to it. Listening to a recording of your voice will help you understand your thoughts in a new way.

Thinking about how to set up your thoughts

The best time to organize your ideas is when you're awake, paying attention to details in the present. You might even have to work hard to give your ideas structure. This may be true, but it's only true sometimes.

You might not know it yet, but there are many passive ways to "arrange" your thoughts. For these methods to work, you must stop consciously processing information and let your subconscious do it instead. If this is your first time, try these methods out since this is an entirely different way to organize your ideas!

Do something you'll have to do again and again

Try doing some things repeatedly to get your thoughts in order. Using your hands frees up your brain to deal with all the thoughts and ideas flooding your mind.

Find something to do that doesn't require much work, either mentally or physically. This could be as simple as putting information from a business card into a spreadsheet, ironing clothes, fixing a button, removing old papers, dusting furniture, filing papers, or getting your desk or room in order.

Choose something you'd like to do and do it! While working, your brain automatically sorts your thoughts and puts them in order.

Stop and think

Meditation calms not only the mind but also the body. It can also help you organize your ideas and put them in order. This method tells you to take it easy and let your mind do the work.

How do you get things going? Turn down the lights or shut the curtains in your room. After that, find a comfortable place to sit, whether a chair, bed, or a pillow on the floor. It would help to sit in a way that makes you feel comfortable.

The next steps are also very simple:

- Sit down and chill out.
- Slowly and calmly, take in and let out the air.
- Stop doing what you're doing and relax for a while. If you meditate often, take a few minutes to relax and keep your attention on your breathing.

Ask yourself again in the morning

Things that seem confusing and chaotic right now will make much more sense in the morning. Getting a good night's sleep can significantly affect how clear and focused your mind is the next day. This method can be beneficial when you need to make a choice or talk about the terms of a deal.

What steps must be taken to put this plan into action? Put on your nightgown and crawl into your cozy bed. Then go to sleep as usual. You'll have a different view in the morning. Try it. It will be fun for you.

Ways to organize your thoughts in the real world

As discussed earlier, it is best to let your mind and body decide how to arrange your thoughts. Sometimes, to find the answers you're looking for, you should "get out of your head." This could mean getting your heart rate up, spending time with other people, or giving yourself a physical challenge to show what you think.

Here are some great ways to physically organize your thoughts. They compel you to get out of your head and show what you think through your body and other people. Try moving your body the next time you desire to get your thoughts in order.

Get out and move

Raise your heart rate and get some exercise. Exercise has numerous positive mental health effects in addition to physical benefits. In terms of exercise, what options do you have?

Try going to the gym, taking a walk with friends, playing fetch with your dog, jogging outside, gardening, or playing tennis with a neighbor.

As I said before, the change of pace will offer your mind a break and let your subconscious work on your puzzle in the background.

Take time to be with nature

Remember the last time you did something enjoyable outside? This is a great chance to see what's close to you, whether 5 or 50 minutes away.

Think about the natural places close to your home or work. For example, you could sit on a park bench, walk a trail in a nature preserve, or look at a beautiful green pasture. You can find great places to visit by doing a little research online.

Put on comfortable shoes for walking or running, clear your mind, and open your eyes to the splendor around you.

. . .

Talk to a friend or member of your family

Even when you've gone over thoughts and concepts in your head, sometimes it helps to talk about things with another person.

Getting things out of your head and off your chest will make you feel much better. A bonus is that a good friend can help you find patterns, make sense of your thoughts, or see things from a different point of view.

Schedule some time to speak with a reliable loved one or friend privately. Friendship also requires being someone to listen to when someone else needs to vent.

Tell a story

Telling a story is a fantastic way to get your thoughts organized. It makes you think about what matters in the story and what doesn't.

You can tell the story in any way you want: telling it, acting it out, putting on a puppet show, drawing or sketching it, making a radio play, or any other way you want.

Start with any one of your ideas and go from there. "At one time..."

Key takeaways

- If you break down your plan into manageable chunks, you can't help but arrive at the correct conclusion. When something isn't immediately apparent, making a list of your thoughts often helps.
- Writing is one of the undemanding ways to organize your thoughts.
- Doing certain activities over and over may help you organize your ideas. Putting your hands to good use allows your mind to focus on the many issues that require attention.

15

PERSUASIVE COMMUNICATION IN
RELATION TO BUSINESS

Have you ever wondered why some people seems to be born with the capacity to influence while others appear to be doomed to spend a lifetime trying to negotiate. How do the rules of society condition us to accept some individuals with little questioning? It's because they can influence others with just their words. This chapter will examine several case studies that demonstrate the efficacy of persuasive writing and public speaking in business. In addition, we will provide a rundown of the most important components of compelling communication as a guideline. It's time to start the festivities.

The goal of persuasion is to influence another person's beliefs or actions about a topic by delivering a message while maintaining our free will. Attractive messengers, persuasive arguments, and an emphasis on the topic's relevance to the recipient's life are just a few elements found in compelling communications. Thus, persuasive communication can be a handy instrument in accomplishing a person's objectives, whether internal or external in the business context.

To build a productive, collaborative working relationship with your teammates is essential so you can communicate effectively and persuasively. The same is true for groups of various ages whose members come from different ethnic backgrounds. You can use persuasive language to communicate your point to your manager or team leader when interacting with them.

In interactions with patrons and customers, the ability to communicate persuasively is used to persuade clients and customers that you're the best person for the job. Exactly why is it crucial for business success to be able to communicate effectively and persuade others?

Entire industries built on the art of persuasion (advertising agencies, marketing companies, public relations firms, etc.) rely on it to make a profit. The average person is subjected to 6,000 and 10,000 advertisements daily, making persuasion widespread. Salespeople are trying to convince you to buy something everywhere you look.

Now that consumers have more options than ever, businesses need to be savvier and creative to persuade them to buy their wares. The art of persuasion has evolved, and now many businesses utilize sophisticated advertisements to convince consumers to buy their services or wares.

With the ever-expanding reach of media like TV, radio, and the internet, it is simpler than ever to convey an argument persuasively. But how can one make the most of persuasive communication in the workplace? Below are instances of persuasive discourse in the workplace:

When you stop to consider it, most things that occur in business settings (the completion of tasks and projects, arriving at conclusions, conduct at business meetings, etc.) are the result of the influence of one person over another.

The key to successfully persuading others lies in your communication skills. Let's look at how specific companies use persuasion in the workplace.

Counterproductive persuasion at work

Example 1:

Shirley runs a successful online marketing firm as its chief executive officer. She is set on implementing a remote-first work approach to cut down on expensive office space. Shirley sends this message without first asking her staff what they want and need.

"CEOs can utilize Facebook to reach out to their entire staff."

Why would this persuasive discourse be unfavorable? She intended to convince her staff to adopt the remote-first approach. Still, her commanding tone ended up having the opposite effect.

Shirley made this sound like an order instead of an explanation by not understanding her audience, not employing the appropriate communication tactics, and not offering supporting reasons. Some workers decided to follow the new policy fearing for their jobs. Some workers left their jobs because they were forced to accept changes against their will.

Example 2:

Gordon works as a human resources manager in a software firm. He plans to introduce a remote-first work style to cut costs for the organization. He polls the staff to see which kind of management they prefer before making any significant moves. Gordon has compiled the data and has decided to send the following message:

"Facebook enables a quick and simple survey of staff members."

Just what are the benefits of this type of persuasive discourse? In contrast to Shirley, Gordon comes across as someone who wants to keep all current employees on board by being transparent about the firm's status and showing that he cherishes employees' thoughts and concerns.

Because of this, he has a better chance than Shirley of recruiting others to join a remote-first business. They won't feel pressured into making a decision, but rather, as though they voluntarily made one. Gordon is better positioned to win over his staff to his proposed adjustments because of his ability to communicate effectively and frame the situation.

Practice the following skills if you want to become an effective persuader:

- EQ, or emotional IQ
- Listening skills
- Logic and reasoning
- Communication abilities
- Competence in bargaining
- Body language

Let's take a close look at the whole list.

EQ, or emotional IQ:
Emotional intelligence (EQ) is the capacity to under-stand and manage one's emotions and those of others and to read and respond appropriately.

Higher EQ is useful in the workplace since it allows for the following:

- relationship-building
- stress-reduction
- conflict resolution
- increased job satisfaction

Being kind is often misunderstood as requiring emotional intelligence. From the standpoint of persuasion, emotional intelligence can help you adjust your communication style to the needs of a particular scenario or person.

Listening skills:

While the term "listening skills" is often used to describe a person's disposition when interacting with others, we will narrow the emphasis to those traits most valued in the workplace.

The following forms of listening should be taken into account:

- To engage in active listening (i.e., listening to comprehend), one must focus entirely on the speaker, pay attention to both their words and body language, and make an effort to respond to what they've said positively. Active listening fosters an atmosphere of two-way comprehension between the speaker and the listener.
- Biased or selective hearing (i.e., listening to pick up certain information): With selective listening,

the person is more intent on filtering the message to take up only the information that can be applied to themselves and their experience.

- Directive listening (also known as "evaluative hearing") is a form of solution-focused or evaluation-based listening in which the listener pays attention to the speaker and offers feedback to guide the speaker in the desired direction.
- High-definition, all-encompassing listening (also known as "listening to relate") permeates all stages of the conversation. When listening attentively, one empathizes with the speaker, considers the context and intensity of the conversation, and pays attention to the speaker's body language, tone of voice, linguistic style, and pauses.

Logic and reason:

Presenting evidence and reasoning that back up your position is vital. The need to foster the ability to think and use logic in conversations. Articulating your thoughts convincingly will serve you well in all interpersonal interactions, so don't hesitate to adopt a logical frame of mind.

Communication abilities:

The capacity to connect with others is exemplified through interpersonal skills. If you want to persuade others with your words, you must come across as authentic, sincere, and charismatic. Developing your people skills ought to be your first concern, and people who connect with you are likely to agree.

Competence in bargaining:

Negotiation and persuasion often go hand in hand. When trying to convince someone to take action, it is best to:

- Recognizing their requirements,
- developing a plan to fulfill those requirements, and
- delivering an arrangement that satisfies all parties involved.

Body language:

Besides verbal exchanges, body language also serve as a means of connecting with new people. Whenever you have contact with another person, you communicate via:

- Changes in facial expression
- Eye blinking
- Physiological stance
- Gestures
- Touch
- Space use

Saying kind things to someone can backfire if your body language belies your sincerity. Unconsciously tapping your foot, for example, indicates show you're uneasy.

According to their level of persuasion, people can be placed into categories:

A professional communicator can persuade others to listen to their message. A person who can persuade others to care about their message is a leading communicator. The ability to persuade an audience to take action is a must for any executive position, and that's exactly what you get with this communicator.

Your ultimate career goal should be to master the art of executive-level communication. Listed below are methods of persuasion that should assist you in reaching your goal. The human brain, a master of manipulation and persuasion, is always on the lookout for quick cuts to:

- Reduce the likelihood of someone becoming overwhelmed, and
- Successfully persuade them to act in a certain way.

Persuasion theory and practice

Humans are obligated to repay those who have shown them kindness by performing an act of kindness or extending them a favor. Most people want more of items in limited supply. Most individuals will follow the recommendations of those they perceive to wield authority. Maintaining continuity with prior statements and actions is highly valued by most individuals.

Cooperation is more likely when people are around others they enjoy, who are alike to them, who complement them, and who work for the same goal. When faced with ambiguity, individuals often look to the actions, beliefs, and attitudes of those around them as "social evidence" to guide their decision-making.

At its core, the concept of unity, which considers the influencer and the influenced common identity, is the human urge to feel a sense of belonging. You can alter your approach to persuading others ethically and effectively by making five relatively minor and usually cost-free adjustments.

Knowing your audience's values, beliefs, and needs is essential before starting any persuasion campaign. Then, you'll need to show them why supporting you and your plan is worthwhile. Consider a humorous anecdote or a fascinating fact that connects to your pitch; the more they know about the subject, the more likely they agree with you.

Lastly, people who can connect with you and have faith in you will likely do more than listen to what you say. Think about where you currently stand as a leader and how you might improve it to be seen as a reliable figure. To what extent are you relied upon by those under you?

Leaders may make a difference if they have an effective communication style. Provide evidence to back up your claim. If you want to persuade someone to accept your point of view, you should back up your claims with solid evidence and specific examples. To convince someone of something, look for evidence to support your claims.

- Make a chart out of the data that matters.
- Create a brochure that describes the advantages.
- Create a poster containing a single thought-provoking question, statement, or quote.
- Create a list of what could go wrong.
- Describe the advantages that everyone will enjoy.

Clearly outlining the benefits you and the other person will enjoy is another strategy for gaining agreement. To come across as credible and trustworthy, it is important to put in the time and effort to prepare thoroughly and thoroughly. Modify your delivery to suit the channel. Tailoring your persuasion message to the medium you intend to employ is important.

Key takeaways

- Facts and numbers are adequate when persuading someone via email or electronic communication. There is ample time for them to read and think about the material you send them in writing.
- It's only sometimes possible to utilize data and evidence to sway someone's opinion when you're having a face-to-face discussion.
- The best strategy for persuasive communication is to make the other person feel "on their side" by emphasizing your shared values and experiences.

16

PROVOKING DESIRE

E agerness to acquire new knowledge is a critical quality that contributes to success in many facets of life. To improve our capacities and boost how we take pleasure in life, all that is asked of us is to maintain an attitude receptive to novel approaches to completing chores, acquiring information, or being entertained.

One must first be willing to adapt to new situations and pursue personal development to learn how to communicate effectively. This chapter will focus on helping you improve your abilities in public speaking, so keep that in mind as you read on. Here are some suggestions for making improvements:

1. It's normal to be worried. Get ready, and put in the work!

Specific physiological responses, such as a speeding heartbeat and trembling hands, are universally experienced by humans. Do not equate these feelings with the worry of giving a terrible performance or embarrassing oneself in front of others. There are good and terrible forms of nerves. Because of the rush of adrenaline that leads you to sweat, you become more aware of your surroundings and better prepared to give your finest performance.

The most effective treatment for anxiety is preparation, preparation, preparation, and even more preparation. Invest time in carefully reading over your notes several times. Once you feel comfortable with the material, put in a lot of work practicing it. Create a video of you performing the task, then ask a buddy to critique it.

2. Understand your market. They, not you, are the focal point of what you have to say.

Before you begin writing your message, give thought to the people reading or hearing it. Discover as much information as possible about these people. This will help you decide on the level of material you want to include, the organizing style you wish to use, and the motivational statement to make.

3. Organize the information to be most helpful in achieving your objectives.

Establish a framework for your presentation. It is important to note the subject matter, the general goal, the precise goal, the main points, and the central thought. Aim to pique the audience's interest within the first thirty seconds of your presentation.

4. Listen carefully to constructive feedback and make necessary changes.

Always keep in mind who you're speaking to. Evaluate their replies, adjust your message, and retain a flexible attitude. Even the most attentive audience members will get disinterested or confused if you present a speech written by someone else.

5. Let your unique individuality come through.

Maintain your authenticity and steer clear of becoming a talking head. Your audience will be more likely to accept what you say and believe in you more strongly if they can relate to you personally. Your credibility will grow if your personality shows through.

6. Relate anecdotes, use witty expressions, and communicate using powerful words.

Suppose you incorporate a funny anecdote in your presentation. Your audience will be more attentive to what have to say. In most cases, audiences are more receptive to presentations that include a personal element in the form of a story.

7. Only read when it's required. Follow your outline.

When someone reads from a script or a PowerPoint presentation, it is detrimental to human interaction. You can keep the audience's attention on you and what you say if you maintain eye contact. You can maintain your focus and stimulate your memory with a brief outline.

8. Make skillful use of both your voice and your hands. Leave out tense gestures.

The vast majority of signals are transmitted in a nonverbal fashion. Effective delivery, however, conveys the speaker's thoughts straightforwardly and inconspicuously instead of bringing attention to the gestures alone.

9. Capture the audience's attention right from the beginning and then keep it throughout the exciting conclusion.

Do you find it interesting when speakers start their talks by saying, "X is the topic we are going to discuss today."? The vast majority of people don't. As an alternative, you may use a surprising statistic, a captivating anecdote, or a short quotation. You should leave your audience with a powerful takeaway from the final portion of your speech, one they will remember.

10. Make judicious use of the various audio-visual aids.

Be careful how often you utilize them because doing you can break your connection with your audience if you use too many. Either they should improve or clarify the material you have provided, or they should catch and keep the interest of your listeners.

Key takeaways

- We can improve our skills and how much we enjoy life by staying open to new ways of doing chores, getting information, or having fun.
- No one expects that you will be error-free, as effective communication will never be flawless. However, the quality of your presentation can be improved by devoting the proper amount of time to preparation.
- You may find it challenging to get rid of your anxiety entirely, but you can learn how to control and live with it.

17

PUBLIC SPEAKING

I t's been said that public speaking is more terrifying to some people than death itself. That may seem a bit radical, but it makes perfect sense. Our forebears were interdependent to stay alive. If you were accepted or rejected by society, it could spell the distinction between life and death. It is rare for people to leave a presentation. It's understandable why many of us find it so frightening. It is the result of our innate drive to stay alive. However, speaking in front of an audience becoming more and more valued in the modern job market.

Read on for advice that will make you a more confident and effective speaker in front of an audience. Success in every field or business venture demands solid verbal communication abilities. According to research by the Association of American Colleges and Universities, most executives and hiring managers value good oral communication abilities. Public speaking is inevitable in most careers, whether a presentation to coworkers or a keynote address at a convention.

Despite this, the survey's participants claimed that fewer than half of recent college grads are adequate at this task. If you want to succeed in public speaking, you must be able to vocalize your thoughts clearly. At the same time, you need to present yourself in a way that makes people care about you. However, many of us suffer from nerves before giving a speech, making it challenging to convey our message and connect with our audience.

Speaking in front of an audience is helpful in many settings, not just the workplace. The fear of public speaking can negatively impact an individual's private life, leading to misunderstandings with loved ones or keeping them from participating in the things they enjoy.

You might, for instance, refrain from sharing your thoughts and goals at a wedding or other social gathering or giving a speech altogether. You may feel that no one gets you when you can't express yourself clearly. Dissatisfaction, isolation, and even dread about interacting with others might result.

Don't feel bad if you get nervous on stage; it's a common problem. Public speaking is a talent that few people are born with. This is encouraging since it suggests that mastery is possible. So, let's get into the steps to take to improve your public speaking skills. There are many practical uses for improved public speaking skills in the workplace. Your self-assurance will increase as a result, too.

Learning to be an excellent public speaker is feasible even if you are naturally shy or suffer from chronic anxiety. Take a look at these four aspects that affect your communication skills.

Manipulation via voice:

You can't get by without your voice, which is why it's the primary tool used to convey ideas. Public speaking skills can be greatly enhanced by mastering the proper application. The use of diaphragmatic breathing to modulate one's voice is highly recommended. If you suffer from anxiety-related breathlessness, this technique may help you speak more clearly and loudly.

To practice this method, allow your tummy to hang loose and become more prominent as you breathe in and out. For a count of four, do not breathe, then exhale for a count of four. Note that the ability to use this breathing effectively while speaking requires practice. In addition, it has a calming effect.

Controlling these three components of your speaking voice with diaphragmatic breathing will help you shine in front of an audience.

- Volume
- Tone
- Pitch

Communication through nonverbal means:

Body language is what you say with your hands, face, and entire body. It's fundamental to the way we interact with one another in the world. It aids the listener in picking up on the subtleties in your message. Your words will only be apparent if your body language is consistent. When you perplex your audience, you lose them forever.

Here are some ways to improve your body language and get your audience interested:

Don't slouch if you can help it; instead, stand up straight. If you want to convey a particular message, your expression must match it. In other words, don't move. The constant motion may alter the way your message is received or even serve as a distraction to your audience.

Get into some confident positions before you give your speech. This will help you feel more at ease and increase your self-esteem. Experiment with a wide stance and an outstretched stance. Try taking a few deep breaths and gauging how you feel after. The best method to learn how to communicate effectively is to observe the body language of those who are good at it.

Delivery:

What we mean by "delivery" is how we express ourselves verbally. A well-delivered speech is vital for communication with the listeners. If you want to make a better impression, try these methods:

- Keep your speech rate at a natural conversational pace. Talking slowly is best, as listeners may need help keeping up. Talk slowly, or they'll lose interest, but don't bog them down.
- Frequent pauses are encouraged, allowing the information to sink in. The effect is one of increased assurance.
- Don't stammer or swallow your words; speak plainly.
- Silence your "ahhs" and "umms" between sentences. Just pause for a second if you need to collect your thoughts. Ten seconds of silence won't hurt anyone.

Audience relation:

Getting folks interested in what you're saying immediately is crucial. Here are some ways to start a dialogue with your niche audience:

- Put on a kind face and shake hands with the spectators. Let them sense how much you appreciate their presence. Doing so will put you in a more approachable light and set a more casual tone.
- Find those listeners who are nodding along with your points. Picture yourself talking to them exclusively.
- Practice making eye contact with as many individuals as you can. This will aid in making your audience feel more connected to you.

Anyone may learn to become an effective public speaker. If you're afraid of public speaking, make sure to make an impact at your next event by following the advice below.

1. Get ready:

Planning is the first step toward delivering a fantastic presentation or speech. Think about the main points you want to make. Look for fascinating facts and data to back up your position. To be ready for any questions that may be asked, you should practice answering them.

Preparing also includes logistical planning. Check out the venue ahead of time to know what to expect. If you need a microphone or a projector, now is the time to give it a shot.

2. Visual aids, such as a PowerPoint presentation, can be pretty helpful. But if it's going to give you additional tension and stress fretting about scrolling through the slides, then don't. Regarding images, there is no ironclad rule.

3. Doing the work:

Get some mirror time or record yourself and play back your speech to see how you're doing. Evaluate your tempo, volume, body language, and expression to spot problem areas.

Find ways to practice your public speaking skills, such as giving presentations at work or signing up for Toastmasters. Prepare for your public speaking opportunity by practicing your speech as often as possible. You can do this in front of the mirror, videotape yourself, or practice in front of friends and family.

4. Keep a sunny disposition:

When putting on a show, nerves are natural. Studies have shown that moderate anxiety might improve results. Try not to allow your anxiety to lead to a downward spiral of despair. Accept it, and then use it as a springboard for increased efficiency. Imagine you've just given the best speech of your life, and use that mental image to help you stay upbeat and confident. Most successful people find that visualizing their data helps them perform better.

5. Engage the listener.

This works double duty as a method of diverting attention away from yourself and getting them interested in something else. Suppose you let an audience member take center stage alongside you. In that case, you'll quickly build rapport and experience less anxiety.

6. Tell a tale.

The human brain is hardwired to focus on narratives. As a result, the same neural circuits are fired as if we were there at the events being re-created.

It's human nature to react to stories in this way, and there is zero cultural variation. That's right; you can use the art of storytelling to strike up a conversation with anyone. One minute is all you have to make a good impression when you first begin speaking, and the audience may be piqued into further attention with a story, anecdote, or query.

7. Dress appropriately:

Looking good can boost your confidence. As a result, high spirits are essential for excelling in one's performance.

Considering this, do you prefer lounging around in pajamas or wearing your favorite suit or dress? You should dress to impress but also in a way that makes you feel at ease. Refrain from surprising people with a new look today. Wearing something that requires continual adjusting will be irritating.

8. Don't pretend to be someone you're not:

It's human nature to model your public speaking style after that of an inspiring public figure. Yet this is a bad idea. No one else can ever truly understand you or your experiences the way you can.

You may wish you were funnier, but you aren't. Not a problem. When you first take the stage, don't start making jokes. Instead, play on your other personality peculiarities (we all have them) in your delivery. It's impossible to tell how many people in the crowd will find your words moving.

9. Solicit comments:

To improve your presentation, have a friend or coworker look it through and give you their honest comments. Likewise, you can record or film yourself. The key is to get them to be as explicit as they can, so tell them to take a close look at your strengths and weaknesses.

Most likely, you have some idea of where you excel and where you may use improvement in public speaking. You will soon master your fear of public speaking and enhance your enhanced skills.

It is possible to conquer your fear of public speaking, even if you are an introvert or suffer from social anxiety. You'll feel better about yourself and could even find that you enjoy it. Take a public speaking course if you still need more information on improving your public speaking. Also, hire a coach to assist you in gaining self-assurance and honing your general speaking skills.

Key takeaways

- To be successful in any field or business, you need to talk to people well.
- You might wish you were funnier, but it's not a big deal if you're not. Don't start making jokes as soon as you get on stage. Instead, use your other quirks to make your delivery more interesting.
- Even if you are shy or have social anxiety, you can overcome your fear of speaking in front of people.

Dear Reader,

As independent authors, it's often difficult to gather reviews compared with much bigger publishers.

Therefore, please leave a review on the platform where you bought this book.

KINDLE:

LEAVE A REVIEW HERE < click here >

Many thanks,

Author Team

CONCLUSION

This book has many chapters, but what can draw from it? The significance of one's words cannot be overstated. If unsure of what you meant, your listeners will likely revisit what you said to ensure they have understood. This means carefully choosing your words, especially when making a significant point. Some considerations:

- The people who will be listening to you. The audience determines the tone and vocabulary used while communicating with others, whether 200 strangers at a conference, a trusted colleague, your employer, or your children. Always remember whom you're talking to and how advanced or novice they might be in the topic before you start talking.
- It's easier to read and comprehend when sentences are shorter. The use of shorter sentences also helps to establish a sense of urgency.

- The use of simpler terms aids in communication. You haven't grasped a concept if you can't break it down and explain it to a child. This is especially crucial if some or all of your readers do not share your native language.

As much as your physical appearance counts, your voice can tell others about your background. One's voice and the words used to express feelings can reveal a lot about mental health.

Hesitation in one's speech, for instance, may be indicative of low self-esteem. A timid individual could mumble, while a self-assured person would talk loudly and clearly. If you have difficulty speaking in front of an audience, try to control your voice, which helps you feel more assured in yourself.

Acclimating yourself to the sound of your voice is essential. Home, or any other private setting where with fewer outside influences and fewer societal norms and expectations is where most people feel most at ease. However, while various factors affect how people communicate, it becomes different in social settings.

Studies have shown that over half of all communication is nonverbal. Verbal, non-verbal cues include tone, speed, and intensity. But how you carry yourself with your body is equally significant. Consider your posture, the expression on your face, the emphasis you add to your words with your hands, and even eye contact.

The chapter "Body Language", provides further information on the topic of efficient communication through the use of non-verbal cues. considerate would help if you considered the distance between you and your audience and whether or not you need to overstate your motions to be understood.

Fidelity is essential for good communication. If you want to convey your point across clearly, your words and body language must be in sync. Since non-verbal cues are more challenging to mask than words, it is best to focus on the latter if you notice inconsistencies between what someone says and how they act.

Because of this, consider your body language and other non-verbal indications. This is even more crucial if you are conveying an unpleasant or challenging message.

All your concerns about effective communication have been covered, and you should now feel more confident in your ability to command an audience.

www.ingramcontent.com/pod-product-compliance
Lightning Source LLC
Chambersburg PA
CBHW020542030426
42337CB00013B/940